HOPE MEADOWS

HOPE
MEADOWS

Real-Life Stories

of Healing and

Caring from an

Inspiring Community

WES SMITH

BERKLEY BOOKS, NEW YORK

A Berkley Book
Published by The Berkley Publishing Group
A division of Penguin Putnam Inc.
375 Hudson Street
New York, New York 10014

This book is an original publication of The Berkley Publishing Group.

Copyright © 2001 by Wes Smith
Jacket and interior photographs by Caroline Greyshock
Text design by Tiffany Kukec

PRINTING HISTORY
Berkley hardcover edition / April 2001

The Penguin Putnam Inc. World Wide Web site address is
http://www.penguinputnam.com

Library of Congress Cataloging-in-Publication Data

Smith, Wes, 1953–
    Hope Meadows : real-life stories of healing and caring from an inspired community /
Wes Smith.
        p. cm.
    ISBN 0-425-17840-4
        1. Hope Meadows (Rantoul, Ill.) 2. Children—Institutional care—Illinois—Rantoul. 3.
Abandoned children—Services for—Illinois—Rantoul. 4. Abused children—Services for—
Illinois—Rantoul. 5. Foster grandparents—Illinois—Rantoul. 6. Intergenerational
relations—Illinois—Rantoul. 7. Intergenerational communication—Illinois—Rantoul. I.
Title.

HV473.R352 H667 2001
362.73'09773'66—dc21

                                                                                    2001018090

PRINTED IN THE UNITED STATES OF AMERICA

10   9   8   7   6   5   4   3   2   1

To the caring men and women who each day give of themselves and their talents to help rebuild broken childhoods within the Hope Meadows community, and to my own parents whose love and support I understand and value now more than ever.

A c k n o w l e d g m e n t s

The families, seniors, and staff of Hope Meadows graciously opened their homes and their lives to me for more than a year of interviews, research, and observation for this book. I'm sorry that not all of their names appear in these pages but all of them deserve my gratitude and that of society as a whole for the difficult work they do in providing guidance and support for young people who otherwise would have little opportunity to thrive.

Brenda Eheart, the founder of Hope Meadows, deservedly gets most of the credit for its successes in this book and elsewhere, but she would be the first to note that the day-to-day operation of Hope Meadows is largely in the capable hands of her administrative assistant, Carolyn Casteel, who guided me through my research with the same skill, care, and diplomacy that she wields within the Hope Meadows community. I am also particularly indebted to University of Illinois sociologist David Hopping who unselfishly shared his research, candor, and insights.

A book that deals with the often cruel realities of abused and neglected children and the failings of the foster-care system is not an easy sell, but my literary agent, Jan Miller, and her staff were also inspired by the stories from this unique child care colony in central Illinois, and I am grateful for their support. Denise Silvestro at The Berkley Publishing Group, a division of Penguin Putnam Inc., became not only my editor but a champion of Hope Meadows, as did Liz Perl, vice president and executive director of publicity at Penguin Putnam Inc., and Craig Burke, assistant director of publicity at Berkley. They were so moved by the stories from Hope's residents that they came to Rantoul to see the community for themselves. It is rare for an author to get that sort of commitment and involvement from his publisher, and I am grateful to them as well.

My thanks also to photographer Carolyn Greyshock, whose portraits have helped bring this book to life.

My own family—my wife, Sarah, and children, Andrew and Jessica—shared me with the Hope Meadows family during the writing of this book. I thank them for their love, support, patience, and willingness to listen to these stories—sometimes more than once.

CONTENTS

Introduction
"A COMMUNITY SO OLD-FASHIONED IT IS NEW."
1

Chapter One
"THE KIDS' NEEDS COME FIRST."
19

Chapter Two
"THERE IS A BETTER LIFE."
39

Chapter Three·
"IT WAS A PLACE FOR SENIORS, AND LOLA GRADUATED."
55

Chapter Four
"HIS CARING CAME THROUGH."
65

Chapter Five
"I DON'T FEEL LIKE I HAD A CHILDHOOD."
81

Chapter Six
"I AM INSANE, REALLY."
93

Contents

Chapter Seven
"I've Watched This Man Come Alive Again."
105

Chapter Eight
"It's Kind of Like *Pleasantville*."
115

Chapter Nine
"I Have Come Home, I Guess."
139

Chapter Ten
"This Is What a Child's Life Is Supposed to Be."
149

Chapter Eleven
"I Feel Like I Fit in Here."
161

Chapter Twelve
"There Is a Lot of Real Chicken Soup Around Here."
171

Chapter Thirteen
"Some Kids Are Survivors."
181

Chapter Fourteen
"This Job Is Never Going to End."
197

"A COMMUNITY

SO OLD-FASHIONED

IT IS NEW."

Eighteen phone calls. Eighteen child care agencies. Eighteen rejections. No one wanted the baby found abandoned in a restroom at Little Company of Mary Hospital in the Chicago suburb of Evergreen Park. Doctors feared the child, who they named Baby Jacob, was born with a crack addiction. They put him on a respiratory monitor, wrapped him in a hospital blanket, and passed him on to the Department of Children and Family Services.

At the time, the state's foster care system was being flooded with 1,000 children a month. No one wanted yet another child in precarious health from an unknown background. After nearly four months of trying unsuccessfully to find the abandoned baby a foster home, the child's caseworker learned of a place created for "unadoptables" like Baby Jacob. In this place, a family was waiting to give the abandoned child what he had never known. Beverly and Larry Gardner had served as foster parents in the past, but they'd grown frustrated with the very system that had rejected Baby Jacob. "We came to Hope Meadows because it got too hard saying goodbye to these kids. We want to give them a permanent home."

*   *   *

We'd been here just a few months when Fran and I were standing at the jewelry counter in Wal-Mart one day and I heard someone say, "Hi, Grandpa!" and the next thing I knew Marquis Calhoun, who was about fourteen years old then, had both arms around my waist and he was hugging me and holding on. There was a black couple I didn't know standing nearby and I heard the black man say, "There ain't no way." He was looking at the little black boy and at me, an old white guy, and saying that. So I turned to him and said, "Oh, yes, there is a way."

At first glance, Hope Meadows appears to be merely another comfortable, middle-class neighborhood of look-alike brick homes in the blue collar, central Illinois town of Rantoul. It could be the setting for a Gap Kids commercial: children of all colors parading around on bicycles, tricycles, and roller blades while an equally diverse mix of parents and elderly neighbors sit sentry in lawn chairs or stand watch behind picture windows with the curtains drawn back. "A community so old-fashioned it is new" was the description Ted Koppel gave Hope Meadows when *Nightline* came to visit, and indeed, the normalcy of it all is underwhelming. This, too, is by design. Like Disney's Celebration in Orlando, this planned community was created for a specific purpose. But the goal at Hope Meadows is not to improve on reality, only to exorcise the most malignant aspects of it—those that would destroy childhoods and forever cripple lives. "Normal is good. Normal is what we want here," says Brenda Eheart, cofounder of Generations of Hope and creator of Hope Meadows. "We don't want these kids to feel different than others. They've already had enough of that."

Each day in this country, 700 children are taken from their parents by court order because of suspected abuse or neglect. Thirty-three percent of those children are never reunited with their parents, nor are they adopted into another permanent home. One-third of those who do go back to their parents eventually re-enter the foster care system, which had responsibility for more than 550,000 of America's children in January 2001. "Often these [children] are held hostage to abuse and neglect, to bureaucratic foul-ups and carelessness, condemned to futures in which dreams cannot come true," *Time* magazine reported in November 2000.

Child welfare laws in Illinois and other states are designed to keep opportunists from profiting from foster care, but scores of nonprofit enterprises have sprung up to meet the soaring demand for foster care facilities. Many of them merely warehouse young people, and society pays the price down the road. All too often, foster homes endanger and corrupt the lives of children rather than enhance them. Federal studies have found that children were killed in state care 5.25 times more often than in their own homes. They were abused three times more while with state care providers than by parents. They are ten to fifteen times more likely to be abused in state care than in their own homes.

"The youth services industry has seen instances of impressive achievement and bright signs of promise. But in numerous cases, personal greed and the financial interests of private companies have been injected into one of government's most sensitive duties: standing in place of failed parents and raising their unwanted children," noted the *Chicago Tribune* in a September 28, 1999, story detailing some of the worst cases of child abuse within the state's nonprofit child welfare agencies.

Although foster care was originally designed to provide temporary emergency guardianship, more and more children enter it as infants or youngsters and remain until they reach adulthood. More than 20,000 children "age out" of the foster care system each year at the ages of eighteen or nineteen, according to the Children's Defense Fund. Nearly 2,000 foster children turned eighteen in the year 2000 just in the state of Illinois. A high percentage of young people who age out of foster care face significant risks of imprisonment, joblessness, welfare dependency, early parenthood, and homelessness. "As any parent of a teenager can attest, the developmental process of growing from adolescence to adulthood is filled with challenges. I believe this is more so for foster children who often feel their entire lives are controlled by external forces such as courts and caseworkers," noted Jess McDonald, Director of the Illinois Department of Children and Family Services in a letter to the *Tribune* on the heels of its investigative report.

The children who suffer the most in foster care are those who need the most help. Often, the most deeply troubled youths are shuttled from one foster home to the next because there are so few foster parents adequately trained to meet their needs. Described in one Congressional report as "America's discarded children," these permanent wards of the state are often afflicted with severe behavioral, emotional, or physical problems. Most of these young people face adult lives of despair unless there is some extraordinary intervention. Many end up in prison, in mental health institutions, on welfare, drug or alcohol dependent, or as suicides. *But for some, there is Hope . . .*

OLDER AMERICANS FACE SIMILAR CHALLENGES

At the opposite end of the generational spectrum, there exists another group of Americans who often feel abandoned and neglected. These are senior citizens, elderly men and women still capable of contributing to society but marginalized by our youth-oriented culture. While the aging of the Baby Boom population is beginning to transform much of the thinking about growing old in America, it is still true that senior citizens are too often put on the shelf and neglected by the rest of society.

The National Council on Aging reports that suicides and murder-suicides involving elderly individuals and couples are rising at an alarming rate, and that depression or poor health is usually to blame. Poverty also contributes to despair among older people. Approximately one third of Americans aged sixty-five or older have incomes just above the poverty line and are unable to afford safe and secure housing. Many of them have led productive lives, but they come to their later years without the security of savings, an adequate retirement fund, or without families willing or able to help care for them. Even those who do have nest eggs and some measure of financial security frequently suffer from social isolation, which research shows can lead to depression, illness, and premature death.

There are countless older Americans who have talents and knowledge to share, many with the willingness and energy to make a contribution, but they feel unwanted by a society that has lost its respect for the wisdom and guidance of its elders. "I was living alone in a little apartment, doing a lot of walking at the mall and thinking there had to be more to life," said retired teacher Irene Bohn.

> But she, and about sixty other seniors, have found hope in a new multigenerational community model that takes the needs of both young and old and transforms them into assets . . .

TWO SOCIAL PROBLEMS, ONE GRASSROOTS APPROACH

For decades, government experts, politicians, and academics have wrestled with these two critical social problems—abused and neglected children, and isolated or "scrap-piled" senior citizens. Child welfare advocates and activists for the elderly have often been pitted against each other in the competition for dwindling public resources and scant funding for human services. There has been a feeling that if one of these age groups is to be served, the other will have to go without. While the bureaucrats and the academics have debated and searched for solutions to these complex and seemingly opposing societal needs, an answer has appeared on the flat and fertile farmlands of the Midwest. It is a deceptively simple approach crafted by an improbable advocate in a most unlikely place.

There are other residential communities for needy children scattered around the country; Boys Town in Nebraska is perhaps the best known. But Hope Meadows, which opened in 1994, is unique in several ways. First of all, it is a healing community created on what was once a military training ground—the former Chanute Air Force Training Base in Rantoul, Illinois.

From 1917 to 1993, more than 2 million men and women were prepared for war and national defense on the 2,400-acre base about 130 miles south of Chicago. Chanute served as a primary training facility for F-111, F-15, and F-16 fighter pilots, and also for the Air Force personnel who operated the Minutemen ICBM missile program. Chanute Field was not a choice assignment for Air Force personnel. Cold winters. Steamy summers. A small, rural community with little in the way of diversions. It became a long-running joke among servicemen that being ordered to Rantoul was the U.S. equivalent of being banished to Siberia. This explains the airman's axiom, "Don't shoot 'em, Chanute 'em."

Today, however, the Hope Meadows neighborhood on twenty-two acres of the former military base is considered a haven, not for America's warriors, but for its neediest children. After the closing of Chanute in 1993, the city of Rantoul worked to convert the base for peaceful purposes. Former bomber hangars now house light industry. The officers' club has been transformed into a popular restaurant. The visiting officers' quarters is a motel. One military dormitory is a retirement home, another is a halfway house for juvenile offenders.

Many of the three-bedroom duplexes that served as married-soldier housing have been converted into six-bedroom, private, single-family homes. But sixty of the buildings were purchased from the Pentagon by Generations of Hope, a nonprofit corporation, funded through a mix of state, federal, and private sources. Currently, twelve "Hope" families live in the homes with thirty-five young people rescued from the child welfare system, and fifteen of their own birth children.

The "special needs" kids who come to Hope Meadows are referred through the Illinois Department of Children and Family Services. Most are either free for adoption or likely to reach that status soon. Newborn infants, teenagers, and children of all ages in between have joined the community. They include children of Caucasian, Hispanic, Asian, African-American, and mixed heritage. Nearly all of the children who come to Hope Meadows from the child welfare system have multiple health and developmental challenges, including asthma, vision problems, cerebral palsy, drug exposure, a history of sexual and physical abuse, attachment disorders, explosive anger, and attention deficit and hyperactivity disorders. A high percentage of them come from broken and severely dysfunctional families. Many are part of sibling groups taken from the same home. Their birth mothers often have histories of mental illness and drug and alcohol abuse. Often, the mothers themselves were abused as children.

A comprehensive assessment of each child's personal and family histories is done upon arrival at Hope Meadows. The information is used to create a strategy and a reference point for the parents and other caregivers. Hope Meadows' approach to child care encourages parents and foster parents to help their children retain ties to their pasts, whether this means staying in touch with birth parents when it is feasible, or placing a blanket from the birth family on the child's bed. "The idea is to help each child understand that they have a history to be valued and built upon," says Brenda Eheart.

The Hope Meadows program is unique also in that the great majority of children who come to it are removed forever from the foster care system and adopted by the resident parents. Currently, the community can house up to fourteen adoptive families. Prospective parents must meet all Illinois State requirements for foster/adoptive parents and Hope parents must agree to adopt up to four special needs children for life. In exchange for that considerable commitment, they pay no housing costs at Hope Meadows. They are also paid a salary of about $19,000 a year so that one parent can stay at home. Several of the Hope parents are single, and most, but not all, work outside the home to supplement their Hope salaries, usually in jobs that allow them to be home when their children are not in school. They are supported by both formal and informal networks within the community. The parents receive weekly training before and after they adopt their Hope children. A child and family therapist lives in the neighborhood, as does an administrative assistant. Both are available around the clock.

ONE GENERATION'S NEEDS BECOME ANOTHER'S SALVATION

Forty-five of the duplexes within the Hope Meadows property were not converted into single-family homes. Instead, these three-bedroom units are reserved for senior citizens—individuals and couples—who live among the adoptive families and serve a vital, supportive role as "foster grandparents" to the children.

There are now nearly sixty of these seniors serving as neighbors, tutors, baby-sitters, crossing guards, playground monitors, bicycle repairmen, mentors, role models, and friends to the parents and their children. Elderly couples and single seniors of all races and income levels have volunteered to contribute to the lives of Hope's young residents. All must undergo criminal background checks and extensive interviews inquiring into their volunteering experience, their interests, abilities, and general health.

The seniors agree to volunteer for at least six hours a week in service to Hope's children and families, in exchange for low monthly rents in the $300 to $400 range—considerably less than the going rate—and for a secure, family-oriented living environment. These older residents very often form deep ties with the families and the boys and girls. Their relationships are symbiotic. The needs of the young serve the needs of the elderly, and vice versa. "I think the reason people become close here is because of the love for the children and the caring for each other; seniors caring for the families and what they're trying to do for the children, and the families caring for the seniors who are trying to help them in any way they can. They know the seniors are here for them and the seniors know that if we need help, there is a family here for us, too," said one Hope foster grandparent.

Hope's multigenerational approach to child welfare generally has worked beyond expectations, according to University of Illinois sociologist David Hopping. "This strategy of combining three or more generations of kinlike support in a secure and welcoming neighborhood has paid off in several ways," noted Hopping, who has studied Hope Meadows since its inception. "Seniors have a safe and affordable place to live, families at last receive adequate support for the often overwhelming task of providing foster care to 'special needs' children, and foster children find an end to (or even avoid) a long series of temporary placements and painful disruptions."

A SINGLE CRUCIBLE AND A MOST PECULIAR ALCHEMY

Hope Meadows "combines overworked foster families, fixed-income seniors, a minimal professional staff, and some of the most egregiously abused and neglected children in the country—yet somehow all parties seem to be thriving," Hopping has found. "Multiple sources of need are combined in a single crucible, and a peculiar alchemy ensues in which needs become resources, resources become multiplied, and certain stubborn costs seem to drop away altogether."

It costs at least $7 billion a year, or about $13,000 per child, just to meet the most basic needs of America's foster kids, according to a *Time* magazine report. Incarcerating a juvenile in Illinois costs an average of $28,000 per inmate. At Hope Meadows, which operates on an annual budget of $700,000, the cost of housing, feeding, and supporting the special needs of each child generally runs less than $20,000 annually.

That's not to say that Hope Meadows is a perfect solution, nor is it a Utopian community free of the conflicts found in other neighborhoods or families. Hope parents, like all parents, can feel overwhelmed and unappreciated. Seniors still can be vulnerable to feelings of loneliness, depression, and the sense that their time may be slipping away. Even the best-intentioned adult may find the demands of such troubled young people too much for them. And not every tormented child can be reached and rehabilitated, even when an entire community extends its arms.

"Calvin," whose real name cannot be given because he is still in the child welfare system, came to Hope Meadows at the age of five. He had already been in five different foster homes. He was placed with a newly arrived young couple who had moved to Hope Meadows to adopt more children, although they'd just had their own first child. Calvin moved in with the couple for a trial period and almost immediately began undergoing mood and behavioral swings. He could be affectionate one minute and venomous the next. He'd offer a hug, and then spit in the faces of his prospective parents. He warmly greeted a foster grandparent, and then made a comment about the size of her breasts.

Calvin's behavior was not all that unusual for a newly arrived child at Hope Meadows. The adult residents are trained to be patient and to work with the children, and, as you will read in the chapters that follow, they have had considerable success in changing such behavior. Calvin was not to be one of their success stories. He told his Hope parents that he was bad and that no one could love him. Worse, he made continual threats that he was going to maim or kill their infant and himself.

Since the records that arrived with him initially had not indicated that Calvin was potentially violent, an investigation was conducted to learn more about the boy's past. When the complete file did arrive, it was several inches thick and full of ominous information. Again, the boy's history was not all that different from many of the children who come to Hope Meadows, but this child, only five years old, had seen too much, and he had been allowed to act out far too long—even at his young age.

His file illuminated the depth of Calvin's unspoken despair. His mother was sixteen when her first child was born. By the time she was twenty-two, she'd had three more children—all by different fathers. Calvin was her second child. The mother did not have a high school degree, and did not work. She reportedly drank heavily, used drugs, was often violent, and rarely stayed in one place very long. She told her state Department of Children and Family Services' caseworkers that she was often overwhelmed by her responsibilities as a parent.

When Calvin was eighteen months old, his younger sister was hospitalized with a skull fracture. When DCFS came to investigate the injury, they found Calvin with a severe burn on his arm. It had not been treated. At that point, there was no electricity in his mother's apartment, and she was on probation. Still, DCFS caseworkers tried to keep the family together; but after eighteen months, they gave up. The mother was unable or unwilling to give the most basic care to her children. All four were taken into protective custody.

Calvin and his older sibling immediately experienced trouble in foster care. They were described as angry and rebellious. They spit at adults, urinated on tables and in mouthwash bottles, and struck other children in their foster homes. That behavior continued when Calvin came to Hope Meadows. He repeatedly threatened his Hope parents and their child with knives. He attempted to cut himself as well. On one occasion, he smeared his own feces all over his bedroom walls, and pulled a mirror from the wall and threw it down the stairs.

Because of the danger Calvin presented to other children and his foster parents, the difficult decision was made to find a place for him outside Hope Meadows, where he could get more extensive treatment. It took thirty-two phone calls to agencies around the state, but finally, two married child welfare professionals accepted him. They have reported that Calvin's violent behavior continues, but they have committed themselves to helping him.

RISK IS PART OF LIFE FOR HOPE FAMILIES

America's child welfare system is vigilant in protecting the privacy of its wards. That protection may be well-intentioned, but it serves to pull a curtain over abuse and neglect that breeds violent, sociopathic, and suicidal adults. In truth, the protected juvenile case files themselves often provide minimal details of a foster child's experiences. Many times, a child's history is deliberately misrepresented, or deleted altogether from his or her file, out of fear that no one will take in a child who is deeply troubled.

As a result, the families of Hope Meadows take a considerable risk when they accept these young people into their homes. The children often arrive here as mysterious packages that have to be handled cautiously, and opened slowly and with great care. Hope Meadows has been home to crack babies and infants born with fetal alcohol syndrome, children with sickle cell anemia and cerebral palsy, siblings rescued from cults, babies burned by cigarettes and clothes irons, pre-adolescent boys who've been sexually abused so long that they crave it, a boy who ate his own feces after being locked alone in a room for days, newborns left so vulnerable from cocaine and alcohol exposure that the sound of a wind chime sets off screams of agony, four-year-olds terrified by the sight of a police squad car, and toddlers left in the care of kindergartners left in the care of third-graders.

Those are some of the stories of the children from Hope Meadows, and so are these:

- A handsome African-American boy taken from a cult family, whose foul language and streetwise manner shocked his Hope neighbors initially. The same child, now adopted, has become a neighborhood charmer, who regularly accompanies his foster grandparents on trips and outings. He recently announced proudly that he had "tested out" of special education classes.

- An adolescent girl once tormented by nightmares from her abusive past, who now dreams peacefully—of becoming an astronaut.

- A round-faced pixie, who was "nearly catatonic" from abuse and neglect as an infant and toddler, but now can't stop talking about the joys of reading the entire *Little House on the Prairie* series.

- A thoughtful and quick-minded teenager who had petitioned the court for removal from her own neglectful family, and recently made the cheerleading squad and the National Honor Society.

- A precocious ten-year-old boy brought to Hope Meadows as a toddler whose parents were both doing prison time on drug charges. Described then by caseworkers as a child who was "failing to thrive," the same child is now lovingly known throughout the neighborhood as "the mayor of Hope Meadows."

A visit to Hope Meadows can be a bittersweet experience. To see so many children being helped is inspiring, yet it triggers the realization that there are so many more in need. This is not the perfect solution for every troubled child, but from the White House to Congress and the United Nations, it has been hailed as one of the most promising models in decades for helping abused and neglected children break the pattern that has afflicted generation after generation. Hope Meadows is not a social service agency, its founder insists. It is more of a communal network of caring relationships. "And those relationships are just very, very powerful. Even I did not see how powerful they would become," said Brenda Eheart.

It is also a living, breathing, ever-changing community of people. Its residents can be fractious, contentious, and downright cranky. Yet, this social experiment has exceeded all expectations so far in reaching children, while also serving the needs of its parents and foster grandparents. Hope Meadows is still developing and metamorphosing. From time to time, residents take its development into their own hands. It is part of the Hope Meadows legend that, early in its history, a group of foster grandparents demanded that one of the duplexes be transformed into a senior citizen center. Brenda Eheart doesn't like to see anything set this neighborhood apart from others. She wants no signs or structures that give it an institutional feel. So, she fought that proposal but she lost the debate. An intergenerational center was created in one of the duplexes. It has become a focal point of the community, a place where young and old and in-between residents gather each day. Seniors hold coffee klatches and bingo parties there. Children work on computers, read in a well-stocked library, and conduct Brownie meetings. Parents meet there and drop their children off with trusted elderly neighbors for a few hours of worry-free errands. Eheart now admits that "the IGC" as it is known, was a terrific idea and a remarkable addition to her model child care community. "I'm glad I was wrong, and I'll probably be wrong again sometime soon," she said.

There will be other tempests within Hope because there always are in constantly evolving communities populated by diverse people. It's too early to tell if this child care colony's central mission of helping abused and neglected children become secure and productive adults has been fully accomplished. It will be many years before most of the young people move on and face adult challenges in the less sheltered outside world. It is certain, though, that they will be hard-pressed to find another place as caring as this, another as densely populated with big-hearted and unselfish individuals.

Hope Meadows provides financial assistance, professional support, and security, but every adult who comes to it makes sacrifices and takes risks in order to serve children in need. Most could live anywhere they desire, but they have come to this unique place in central Illinois for the children. None of the people here are saints. They are as flawed and human as anyone who holds this book in hand. But the parents and seniors at Hope Meadows have stepped up to serve one of society's most pressing needs. For that alone, they deserve recognition as well as our gratitude. And so, I've interviewed them and in a few cases, I've incorporated material from interviews conducted by the staff at Hope Meadows. While most of their stories are ultimately inspiring, some may disturb you in their emotional rawness, or in their frankness. Most will move you, as they have moved me in the six years that I've been familiar with this extraordinary place since first writing about it in 1996 as a national correspondent for the *Chicago Tribune*.

At the very least, their candid reflections provide an unfiltered look into the realities of abused and neglected children, and into those of aging Americans, too. I think, though, that you will find far more. In a world that often seems self-absorbed and hard-hearted beyond belief, it restores your faith in humanity to find that there are still people who believe they can make things better by reaching out and giving of their talents and their time. In spite of all of their differences, the people in this community—young and old, black, white, Hispanic, Asian—work together to salvage shattered young lives, to try and make these damaged children whole again.

Please note: The names and case histories of children who have been adopted by Hope Meadows families are used throughout the book only with their adoptive parents' permission. In some cases, however, names and other information regarding their backgrounds have been altered to protect the privacy of the children or their parents or guardians. The names of children who were still in foster care at the time of the writing of this book have either been changed or not given in order to protect the privacy of juveniles in state care.

—Wes Smith

Chapter One

"THE KIDS' NEEDS
COME FIRST."

The squalid apartment in the Cabrini Green housing project was decidedly unfamiliar territory for a dairy farmer's daughter from western New York. It was 1968. Brenda Krause was fresh out of college with a degree in home economics, and newly hired as a caseworker for the city of Chicago's public welfare office. Her job was to teach child care, budget management, and homemaking skills to welfare recipients. But it was she who received an education—into urban poverty and the plight of America's neglected and abused children.

I remember entering this apartment and going down this long, dark hallway with no windows, and cockroaches everywhere. In the very back, there was a crib just reeking of urine. There was a baby in the crib. I remember feeling despair, and thinking, "How can this child survive in this environment? How is his brain going to develop normally? How will he ever have any chance in life?"

That night I called my mother, who'd spent her whole life on the family farm. She was terrified that I was working in the ghetto. I cried with her on the phone about that baby, because I felt there was no way to help that child. That was when I began having a deep interest in these kids.

I take it personally when I see kids mistreated. I just think they need an advocate to fight for them, and when people in the child welfare system are not willing to do that, I don't understand it. For me, it's very simple: The kids' needs come first. That's the bottom line at Hope Meadows. We make decisions as if these are our own children, and when you think that way, your decisions are different than if you are just trying to work within a bureaucratic system.

At fifty-five, this trim, brown-haired woman is a most unlikely crusader and pioneer in child welfare. Brenda was a farm girl from Basom, a village of only 100 residents in the far western corner of New York State. Even her name rings of rural domesticity, 4-H Club, and big family dinners at noon. "I was a home economist," Brenda Krause Eheart concedes. "I really fit the mold." In truth, she has broken the mold. The founder of Hope Meadows is an academic who has become an activist. She is a woman who trained to become a dispassionate social scientist, yet never lost her social conscience. Even now, she finds it difficult to talk about the backgrounds of the children within the community she created without shedding tears.

Eheart's childhood was very much in line with the Norman Rockwell image for rural American family life. And today, her unique, multigenerational model for child welfare is rooted in those traditions. Within Hope Meadows, adults provide a secure, supportive environment for children whose needs are given a high priority. Brenda, her twin brother, and an older sister worked on the farm alongside their parents and a widowed grandfather who lived next door and joined them every night for supper. Brenda drove the tractor that pulled the hay rack while her father, grandfather, brother, and neighbors baled freshly cut hay. Her mother led the local 4-H Club that she and her sister, now a fiber artist, belonged to all through school. There was no generation gap. There was always a support network.

Brenda had a steady high school boyfriend who she planned to marry and spend the rest of her life with in Basom. After earning her undergraduate degree nearby at the State University College of New York at Buffalo, she was on course to fulfill the goal of "mother and schoolteacher" recorded in her 1962 high school yearbook. She had an offer to teach in a local school, and her life appeared to be set and secure if that was what she wanted. But Brenda and the boyfriend broke up, and her mother, who had sometimes longed for a wider range of experience in her own life, encouraged Brenda to see some of the world.

So, her path followed a much different course, beginning with her first job as a dietitian with the Stouffer's food company in Chicago. She worked there for about a year before deciding that she was ill-suited for corporate life. Contemplating a return to school for an advanced degree, Brenda took a six-month position that seemed safe and sensible, as a home economist for Cook County.

One of her first assignments was helping a group of welfare recipients sew white prayer robes; another, however, involved relocating residents of a four-story South Side apartment building that had been burned down for the insurance money. The arson was obvious, Brenda said, since all of the residents, including a bedridden elderly woman, were warned to get out, and did. "That's when I began to realize that the world was not quite as rosy as I'd seen it up to that point," she recalled.

It was the late 1960s and that was when my farm girl's social consciousness was really raised. I was twenty-three years old and I thought, "This can't be happening." I kept a diary while I was working there and about a year ago I found it when I was cleaning. I was astounded at the things I was writing then, my outrage and the influence it has had on what I've done since. The job with Cook County was certainly my first exposure to inner-city poverty, and to the lives of children born in that environment.

In Chicago, she met and married Wayland Eheart, a chemical engineer working as a troubleshooter in oil refinery construction. She put her plans for an advanced degree on hold for the next two years as Wayland's job took them around the world. They traveled throughout Europe and South America, and then, hoping to start a family, they opted for a less nomadic life.

An avid hiker and outdoorsman, Wayland's interests had shifted from the economic aspects of engineering to the environmental. He enrolled at the University of Wisconsin in Madison to get his Ph.D. in environmental engineering. Brenda completed her master's degree in home economics and earned a Ph.D. in the area of child development. While Brenda was working on her doctorate, she gave birth to her daughter, Sarah, now a teacher for behaviorally disturbed children in San Francisco.

The couple completed their course work and earned their degrees in six years. They then moved to Philadelphia, where Wayland taught at Drexel University. Brenda became the instructor of an undergraduate course in child care at Temple University, and mentored her black, inner-city students as they interned with federal child welfare programs such as Head Start. During this period, she and Wayland also adopted Seth, a Peruvian Incan orphan. Their experiences with Seth, and their involvement with other parents with adopted children rekindled Brenda's interest in child welfare and the challenges of being an adoptive parent.

When Wayland took a job as an environmental engineering professor at the University of Illinois in Urbana, Brenda joined the faculty as director of an interdisciplinary program that placed student interns into jobs in the child welfare system. She and another professor, Martha Bauman Power, also spent seven years closely documenting the experiences of families who attempted to adopt and nurture "special needs" children—generally older children with emotional, developmental, or physical problems; minority children; or children from a sibling group. Most of these children experienced deprivation, physical and sexual abuse, abandonment, and many moves within the foster care system.

Eheart and Power worked with nearly a dozen families, and they found that many of the adoptions failed. The adoptive parents were unable to handle the deeply rooted problems of the most troubled young people. These "unadoptable" children were often institutionalized for their entire childhoods, and then sent into the world as adults destined for prison, welfare, or lives on the deadly edges of society.

The two women didn't just study the activities of the foster kids and their families. They all but lived with them, developing an intimate understanding of their frustrations and fears. They concluded from their study that if special needs children are to be salvaged from the foster care system and placed in permanent foster or adoptive homes, their adult guardians needed more support than was normally available. Too often, they found, adoption was a path to disillusionment. Adoptive parents were not provided with complete medical or behavioral histories of the children they adopted, in part because the kids were bounced around so much, there was no continuity of care. As a result the children's needs went unserved. Even today, Eheart frequently gets calls from parents who feel that they've gotten in over their heads after adopting toddlers who mature into terrors because of unknown things that happened to them in their earliest months and years of life, she said.

It makes you think we could be sitting on a time bomb, with all of these explosive kids in foster care and in adoptive homes. These kids come out of abuse and neglect and they are very angry. They should be angry. But to help them work it out is tough if you don't have a complete history.

Working, living, and writing about those children and their families, while also raising my own daughter and son, was really a turning point for me. One of the children we studied shared my daughter's birthday. Others reminded me of my son. I kept thinking, "These could be *my* kids." We really became involved in the lives of those kids we studied. We followed one family when they went to court to terminate their adoption of a nine-year-old boy who'd been adopted after spending years in foster care. They couldn't handle him. Oh God, they terminated their rights and then he became suicidal. He went into a residential center, and wrote letters to the family threatening suicide. It was so sad. We saw so much. Poverty. Low-functioning mothers. A lot of abuse. Families moving constantly. Total chaos for the kids.

I kept thinking there had to be a better way. I knew from my studies and from my instincts that kids need stability and a reliable support system. They don't need to be set apart. They don't need to be moved from one place to the next. I wanted for them what I'd want for my own kids if something were to happen to Wayland and me. I had the basic model, that was simple enough, but I had no idea how it could be turned into a reality.

As Eheart and Power studied the lives of children in the foster care system, there was a growing national debate over child welfare. In the 1970s and into the 1980s, the number of children in foster care rose alarmingly as crack cocaine, economic recession, and cities in crisis tore at the family structure. More and more children were pouring in, and fewer were coming out. Cries for reform reached Washington, D.C., where then–Speaker of the House Newt Gingrich was among those calling for the creation of government-run orphanages to house the thousands of children entering the system each month.

The talk of warehousing needy young people in orphanages "put me over the edge," Eheart said. She felt increasing urgency to find a better alternative. She wasn't alone. All around her, other adoptive parents, social workers, child welfare professionals, foster families, lawyers, and academics were growing alarmed. She became part of a group of concerned central Illinois residents who met regularly to discuss alternatives and formulate strategy. "Drug-exposed babies were being featured on the covers of *Time* and *Newsweek* and that was on everybody's mind. There was a real interest in taking those children out of the foster care system," Eheart said. "We wanted to provide for kids that nobody else would take, including sibling groups, and kids who have been tossed and tossed and tossed around the system."

Most of them agreed that children in foster care need stability and a consistent, nurturing relationship with at least one adult. They also agreed that parents who take in special needs children must have considerable support within easy reach. That support should include trained therapists and child welfare professionals, and also some sort of extended family network. Eheart came up with a vital component of Hope Meadows's support team while attending a speech given by Maggie Kuhn, the founder of the Gray Panthers.

"She talked about a program where seniors could stay in their own homes rather than going into nursing homes, with the help of college students who looked after their needs," Eheart recalled. "After hearing her, a light went on in my mind."

Eheart and her friends developed a concept whereby senior citizen volunteers would be recruited to live among the families in their child care colony. They would then support the parents there, by acting as "foster grandparents" to the troubled young people—in much the same way that Eheart's grandfather served in support of her parents on the farm.

Coming up with a theoretical model was relatively easy. Funding and building it was a daunting challenge. Eheart and her circle of concerned friends had no political clout. No money. No bricks and mortar to build upon. For two years, their grassroots effort seemed unworkable economically, politically, socially, and otherwise. From time to time, they'd learn of properties that might suit their purpose, but they didn't have the means to acquire them. It seemed an impossible dream, until one day in January of 1992, when Eheart was contacted by a U.S. Air Force officer at the Chanute Air Force Base in Rantoul, just twenty miles south of the Urbana campus. The 2,400-acre base was to be closed due to Pentagon cutbacks. The officer had the seeds of an idea about using some of the former military housing to create a residential community for children along the lines of Boys Town. The woman officer had contacted the state's Department of Children and Family Services, and someone within that bureaucracy remembered a university professor with her own ideas about a new type of child welfare.

After touring the property, Eheart had grand dreams of it being donated to her nonprofit foundation within a few months. Those fantasies were quickly dissipated by the local power broker she went to for assistance. "When she [Brenda] first sat down in my office and started telling me about her plans, I thought, 'Oh horseshit, here we go again, another flaming liberal with a pie-in-the-sky concept,'" recalled attorney John Hirschfeld, who served three terms as a state representative, and also held the position of Republican Party chairman in Champaign County.

It was an interesting confrontation. She is a liberal Democrat. I am a conservative Republican. Brenda told me up front that she just wanted to use my experience and contacts. She said she had never voted for me, and that she never liked me much based on what she'd read and heard about me. I thought, "I sort of like this woman." She was no shrinking violet. I don't like people who are easily intimidated. Still, I intended only to talk with her a little while and then kick her out of my office, saying I was retired from politics and didn't have the clout she thought I had.

But as she talked, I got intrigued. I'd throw a barb out and she'd respond with something of her own. The fifteen-minute meeting blossomed into a two-hour conversation. And into an unusual friendship.

Although he would eventually help Eheart put together a diverse coalition of supporters for her groundbreaking child care community, Hirschfeld, sixty-two, seemed at first to be an unlikely ally. Before his retirement from his law firm in 2000, he was a controversial figure in central Illinois. He'd hosted a radio talk show and written a newspaper column in which he often lambasted liberals and other political and philosophical foes.

But the Notre Dame graduate and father of seven had long shown a deep and abiding interest in child welfare. He built his law firm from a one-man office to a staff of twenty primarily on the strength of his adoption law practice, much of it done for Catholic Social Services. Hirschfeld has performed legal work on thousands of adoptions in the U.S. and overseas. He was a founding member of the American Academy of Adoption Attorneys, and, over the years, has helped write and reform state adoption laws. He was not happy with the child welfare system and he found Brenda Eheart's approach intriguing.

The lawyer and former politician came to see Eheart as "a visionary" who was "malleable—as long as you use a hammer."

When Brenda came to me she had stars in her eyes and I tried to get her to be more realistic, but I was all for what she was trying to do. Illinois child welfare is a shambles at best. I was not at all happy with many of the state's agencies and their regulations on child welfare. The law says everything is supposed to be done in the best interests of the child. But that's not how it is working.

I was particularly unhappy with foster care, in which children are shipped from household to household and warehoused. There are good child agencies and good foster homes, but my experience is that far too many foster parents were in it because they were being paid, not because they loved kids. Brenda's concept was to provide permanency for the kids. I don't know if it will answer all the problems, but it is a step in the right direction. I told her that I would do all of her legal work pro bono, but that she was going to need a lot of help politically.

Brenda realized she would need state money to purchase the surplus federal property on the old Air Force base, and the support of state agencies that govern child welfare. So, her next stop was the state capital in Springfield. Her goal was to get at least $2 million in initial state funding. To help her secure the money, Eheart recruited Betsy Mitchell, a forty-six-year-old veteran of 20 years as a lobbyist who she'd known as a volunteer on adoption issues.

When they first met, Mitchell told Eheart she was in for a tough fight. It was already late in the 1993 budgeting session, and then-Governor Jim Edgar was on a cost-cutting binge. Word had come down that no new programs would be funded. Aside from the political issues, Mitchell had a personal problem with Eheart's strategy. "When she told me that I'd have to work with John Hirschfeld, I stood up and said, 'There's no way,' " Mitchell recalled.

I have worked with a lot of Republicans, but I'm actually a Democrat in Republican clothing myself. A Lincoln Republican. I only knew John by reputation. I said, "No, no, no." I told her that she was at opposite ends of the political spectrum from him and that it would never work. But before I knew it, we were all in a meeting together and I found myself serving as the mediator between Brenda and John. It was a fascinating experience. We all fell in love with Brenda's program. She was relentless when we started making the rounds to try to sell it to the legislators. She'd buttonhole legislators in the corridors and chisel away at them. She wouldn't get embarrassed if they didn't listen to her. She'd just keep talking about the kids and what they needed and slowly they'd begin to listen to her.

I'll always remember when she and John came to the first health committee hearing. The committee chairman said that they had more than fifty bills to consider along with Brenda's. He gave them five minutes each to speak. John is a former legislator and a member of the old

boys' club, so they were willing to listen to him. But Brenda was a political neophyte. We were concerned that they would tune her out. She was
marvelous, as it turned out. She and John ended up speaking for about
forty minutes until the chairman finally cut them off and said, "I don't
think we need to hear anymore." John was worried about what that
meant. But all the committee members said it was a great idea. The bill
was passed unanimously out of the committee.

To get the financing bill for Hope Meadows approved by the entire
state legislature so late in the game, Eheart and her improbable
band of Democrats, Republicans, liberals, conservatives, and other
allies went to work. They had to convince key legislators and the
Department of Children and Family Services to support them, or at
least not to fight them. Some child welfare bureaucrats within state
government feared that their funding would be cut to provide money
for this experimental program, so assurances and concessions had
to be made. In the end, their request was cut in half—to $1 million—
and it was a one-time-only appropriation as a special addition to the
budget.

Eheart had her start-up money, but the battle had just begun.
It had been nearly two years since she'd first toured the Chanute
Field properties. She'd been wrestling with the military bureaucracy
since then. The Pentagon, she discovered, had never before
approved the sale of surplus military property to a nonprofit organization. There was no precedent. There were no written procedures.
When the military bureaucracy doesn't have guidelines, things tend
to get slogged down in miles and miles of red tape, she discovered.

For two years, Brenda and her supporters fought for clearance
to purchase housing units on the shuttered base in Rantoul. She was
growing fed up and angry. In a classic, "What the hell, it couldn't

hurt" gesture, she fired off a fax to President Bill Clinton. "It said that he had come into office promising to end gridlock in the federal government but we were mired in it," she recalled. "I also told everyone to start spreading the word that we were asking for a federal inquiry into the whole thing." She got no immediate response from the White House. But to her amazement, the gates of the Pentagon suddenly opened. She won authorization to negotiate the price of the properties she wanted. In September of 1993, she and her nonprofit corporation purchased the duplexes and twenty-two acres within the former air base for $215,000.

In the spring of 1994, the first Hope families moved into the renovated housing. Four months later, the first child from the foster care system arrived to live there with a family. By the summer of the year 2000, Hope Meadows had taken in more than sixty special needs children. Nearly ninety percent have stayed out of the foster care system, with most finding permanent homes with Hope families or their own relatives.

In November of 1998, Hope Meadows and its creator received an Excellence in Adoption Award from President Clinton at the White House. Many other accolades have followed. Hope Meadows was featured on two *Oprah* shows in the summer of 2000. The talk show hostess called Eheart's alternative to the traditional child welfare system a "true haven for the lonely and forgotten" and a place where "the blending of young foster children and aging adults has created a real community filled with hope." Oprah's Angel Network presented Hope Meadows with a $50,000 grant underwritten by actor Paul Newman's charitable foundation.

Although it has been hailed in the media, widely honored, and viewed as a model for the future of child welfare, Hope Meadows's continued existence is not guaranteed by any means. The state of

Illinois still funds it only on a year-to-year basis and it is difficult for Eheart to be both a lobbyist and a care-provider. To ease financial concerns, she has undertaken a $10 million fund-raising effort to create a permanent endowment. In the meantime, organizations, individuals, and government groups interested in replicating her model in other parts of the country are continually knocking on her door. Two years ago, the McDonald's Corporation's Ronald McDonald Foundation offered $8 million as seed money for a nationwide program to replicate Hope Meadows under its corporate umbrella. After the first replication site was identified and developed in urban Cleveland, Eheart and the corporation's liasons agreed that perhaps they'd been too ambitious too soon with their model for child welfare. Eheart feared that the children's needs would not be well served until the model was more developed. The partnership was dissolved, but Brenda is currently weighing several other replication proposals. The creator of Hope Meadows has concerns that she may not have the physical energy to do it, but she feels morally compelled to help as many children as possible escape the systematic cruelty and injustices of the existing approach to child welfare.

In some ways, I find myself an outlaw and I don't really like being an outlaw, but for me, it's just common sense that the kids' needs have to come first. I want to make sure I'm doing that for the kids we already have and will continue to have here in Rantoul before I try to replicate this model somewhere else. A heck of a lot will depend on how much energy I have. There are days when I'm really excited about replication, and days when I don't know if I could handle it if the work is anywhere near as intense as the last six years have been. Some days, I think we've done pretty well to have taken this many kids out of the foster care system and given them back their childhoods. Certain people have convinced me, though, that we have a moral obligation to keep doing this, and to try it in other parts of the country.

Eheart tries to maintain a dispassionate, professional decorum when talking about her work. At first impression, she can appear to be an aloof academic, but it is a thin shield she puts up to protect herself from betraying that she cares so deeply. She is far more vulnerable than she likes to let on, her friends say. In 1984, five years before Hope Meadows was conceived, Eheart was diagnosed with advanced breast cancer. It is painful for her to talk about her extended battle with it, and she said her victory over the deadly disease had nothing to do with the creation of Hope Meadows. But her reflections on that traumatic period of her life do say something about who she is, and how much she cares.

I really hate the fact that I had cancer. I hate that I was so helpless in so many ways and dependent on so many people. It goes so much against how I see myself. And I hate how much my being sick caused those I love to feel pain and anxiety. My anxiety was that I would not get to see my kids grow up. I wanted nothing more than that, and to not have that opportunity was terrifying. Maybe that is why I have so much empathy for birth parents, and these children.

I've come to believe that these kids need what all kids need: a sense of security, the knowledge that somebody will always be there for them. When they come to us from foster care, or out of abuse and neglect, they don't have that. Often, they don't feel secure until they are adopted, and even then their insecurities can easily arise. Before they can heal, they need to know that they belong to a community that cares about them. We give them a community of care in the present, so they will have the memories needed to give and receive care in the future. At Hope Meadows, they have not only their parents and siblings, and other kids from similar backgrounds, but grandparents next door, and an office staff that cares about them and works as a partner with the families.

One of the things I've learned is that children, and really all of us, need to experience random acts of caring in our day-to-day lives. We need to be assured and acknowledged in serendipitous and unexpected ways. The seniors at Hope talk about their spirits being suddenly lifted by the sound of a child shouting out, "Hi, Grandma!" or "Hi, Grandpa!" You hear, too, about deeply troubled kids responding to the simplest and most basic acts of caring, whether it's a tutor trying to help them learn, or a parent showing them how to shoot a basketball. Random acts of caring are vital to all of us, but especially to these kids, who often have never received the clear message that they are loved and that they matter. Here, they can get it from their parents, their siblings, their elderly neighbors, from everyone around them.

In five years, we have become a community with our own history and our own traditions—summer barbecues, holiday parties, and annual trips to places like Washington, D.C., and New York City. I think these kids need that sense of community. It's not a perfect place, but it is a place where they can heal and grow. You know, we have had parents and foster grandparents here who grew up in foster care themselves and they talk about how they've struggled to overcome the sense of isolation and being unloved. I don't know how somebody raised in institutional care without role models or family relationships overcomes that and becomes an adult capable of having lasting and loving family bonds. Those of us who grew up with it take it for granted, but every day, we fall back on our childhood experiences and the values that were formed then. It really shapes us. And if you don't have a foundation, you are forced to try and create one. Some people succeed in doing that. But I think it makes life much harder. The greatest reward for me is knowing that we are helping people build relationships that nourish them—not only the kids, but the seniors and parents, too.

In 1997, Brenda Eheart was named one of *Ms.* magazine's Women of the Year "for creating a better life for foster children and a new vision of community." She is not comfortable with such recognition, nor does she consider herself a role model or heroine. Always, she wants the focus to be on the needy children to whom she has dedicated her life.

I am not any better or worse than someone who chooses to stay home every day and read books and garden. I know it is the "in" thing to say that we should all be giving something back to make the world a better place. I guess I don't believe that. I think everyone should, if they are lucky, do what they truly enjoy doing, whether it makes a difference for others or not. I was able to start Hope because my mother raised me to believe that I could do anything I really wanted to do, and I inherited from my father the ability to be comfortable with and talk to almost anyone. I also inherited a stubborn streak from him. This streak came in handy when I was fighting the Pentagon.

If I could inspire others—and I'm not sure I can—I would like to see everyone try harder to live by the Golden Rule, as trite as that may sound. We try to do this at Hope when we think of our Hope kids and ask, "What would we want for our own children?" I think that would truly make the world better.

Chapter Two

"THERE IS A BETTER LIFE."

Strutting six-year-old Brandon and Shamon, his seven-year-old sister, were streetwise beyond their years when Jeanette Laws agreed to give them a temporary foster home. The two beautiful but troubled African-American children had been taken from their birth mother, a drug abuser diagnosed with multiple personality disorders. A few years before, the mother and children had fled a cult in another part of the country. The mother had belonged to it since childhood and she'd become deeply disturbed. She did not want her own children to suffer the same fate, so she stole them away, hitchhiked with them for hundreds of miles, and brought them to central Illinois in search of safety.

It is suspected that Brandon and Shamon were exposed to cult activity, and possibly abused in it. When they came under Laws's care, the brother and sister were defiant, but also fearful. They trusted no one. Shamon was terrified by recurrent dreams in which "monsters" came to take her away, and blood ran from walls. The child slept only when Laws sat in the room with her, and then only after she checked under her bed and in the closets.

The children's birth mother had taken them from the cult because she was concerned about their well-being, but she could not escape her own demons. At first, when case workers talked to her about giving up her children, she threatened to kill them and to commit suicide so they would all be together in death. But once she was treated for her medical disorder, she began to act more reasonably. She realized she was unable to care for her children adequately, and she became more willing to send her children to a better place.

Jeanette Laws did not vilify the children's birth mother. Nor did she attempt to keep her children from her. Instead, she developed a bond with the troubled woman and won her confidence and trust. When the Department of Children and Family Services moved to have the court terminate the mother's parental rights for Brandon and Shamon, she agreed to give them up, but only if Jeanette Laws would adopt them permanently. Now the children have two women and an entire community devoted to their care. "Their mother loves them, but she can't take care of them. With the help of God and others, I can," said Laws.

When their mother gave them up for adoption to me, I promised her that I would never keep them away from her and I haven't. She still sees them. I try to keep the adoption open so the mystique doesn't affect them; I tell them they don't have to ever search for their mom, they know where she is. They have empathy for her. They feel sorry for her and they ask me to do things for her all the time. I've told them that I can't adopt her, too. Of course, Brandon says, "Why not?"

People think that because children are adopted, all of the adjustment is done, but every so often, when certain things take place, things from their past come back up and you have to deal with it. If their mother doesn't call for a long period, it tends to bother them and they have to find someone to blame for that. Normally, it is the person who happens to be there at the moment—me.

One day, they started in on me and I said, "Listen, I am really sorry for whatever you went through, for whatever took place in your life. I am sorry because you are not with your [birth] mom. I am sorry because you don't know who your dad is. I'm sorry. I'm sorry. If I could change those things in your life, I would. But I can't. However, I will *not* allow you to hold me responsible for what happened before you came to me. I didn't do it. So, you will not blame me for what went wrong in your life. I can't make it right because it is already done. I am trying to help you see that what happened to you in the past is not what life has to be for you. There is a better life."

I don't want them to ever feel that because of the bad things that have happened in their lives that anyone owes them anything. I tell them that they have to make the best out of life that they possibly can and not let the worst of it become a part of them.

Other adult residents of Hope Meadows describe Jeanette Laws, fifty-four, as a "powerful woman." She certainly is that. She runs an alternative high school for troubled teens in Urbana with a strong hand and a compassionate heart, and she brings the same tough-love approach to parenting the children under her care.

In the spring of 2000, this single mother was preparing to do battle on behalf of two more siblings who came to her from foster care. She had hired a lawyer, at her own expense, to help in her efforts to win permanent custody of one of them, a nineteen-month-old boy, whose adoption was being contested by a relative of the child. DCFS took this boy and his infant brother from their drug-addicted mother, who'd already delivered seven children into the foster care system. She and the boys' father were both in and out of jail.

Laws had nurtured other cocaine and crack babies. She agreed to give the two boys a temporary home. She then spent two exhausting months nursing the drug-addicted baby through cocaine withdrawal. "He was in intensive care for seven days before they brought him to me. But it wasn't over. He had terrible tremors, and he would knot up into a ball and scream with sweat just pouring off of him. I could hardly stand to see it," she recalled.

Although she'd been asked to take the boys only on a temporary basis, Laws quickly became attached to them. She decided to adopt both of the children, but her plans were challenged by the boys' uncle. The uncle is a minister who briefly had custody of the oldest child, and now wanted to adopt him but not his younger brother. "The irony is that I genuinely think a lot of him and we have a wonderful relationship," Laws said of the uncle. But she wanted to keep the siblings together and in her care. Her attorney predicted that a contested adoption could cost more than $10,000.

Laws recently cut her work hours to spend more time with her children. Her income dropped to about $22,000 a year. To pay the lawyer's up-front fee, she was forced to take $3,000 from an education fund she had established for Brandon and Shamon. "I talked to the other kids about using the money from their college fund, and we decided to cash it in and go for it," she said. "I don't know how it's going to go. When it comes to these kids and the courts, I am never surprised anymore. I've learned not to say, 'Oh, that couldn't happen.'" (Ultimately an amicable settlement was reached and Laws got custody of the oldest child.)

Being a single mother is challenging under any circumstances. As one with a heart open to children whose own parents have failed them, Jeanette Laws has to scramble to get by, even in the supportive environment of Hope Meadows. "It is a struggle financially, and otherwise," she acknowledged. "But my trust is in God."

There are some days when I don't want to go to work. And there are days when I am so physically tired and emotionally drained from dealing with the kids in school that, if I could, I'd come home, go upstairs, go to my room, close the door, turn on the TV, and go to bed. But I can't do that because I have little people. The kids will say, "You look tired, Mom, we'll cook dinner," but my love for them gives me the strength to do it.

We don't pay rent here, which helps, but we do pay utilities, and, now that I have a baby again, I need to keep working just to pay for the Pampers. I figure I will have to struggle for a few years as a result of working reduced hours but I want to be home more for them, to bring some stability into their lives. That way, I won't have to worry so much when they get older. My mom and dad both worked, but somehow they brought as much stability to our lives as we needed to become functioning adults with our heads on straight. I learned from that.

Laws grew up in Providence, Rhode Island, in a family of seven governed by her "extremely strict" parents. "They taught us that the greatest thing we could do was to watch out for and love each other," she said. Laws has been nurturing children most of her life. She worked with young people in her hometown and in Boston, New York City, and Washington, D.C., before moving to central Illinois about twenty-five years ago when a minister friend asked her to help with the congregation at the Greater Holy Temple church in Champaign.

She was actively involved in that church and in the community when
Hope Meadows recruited her shortly after it opened in 1994.

I was working at the Storefront School and serving on all these local
committees and organizations like United Way, and others having to do
with young people, when my phone rang and a lady said that I'd been
recommended for something else. I thought, "Oh God, not another committee, I don't have an extra moment." But the caller was from Hope
Meadows. She wanted to talk to me about becoming a parent there. We
met and talked for three straight hours about the plight of children, and
she lit a fire in my soul.

In the beginning, I wanted some time to learn more about what
they were doing, so I served as an advocate for the seniors and helped
with their concerns, and I did emergency care for children who needed a
place to stay before going somewhere else. The DCFS would call and say
they had two kids at the police station or elsewhere, and they'd bring
them to me for a few days. I had about eight children in and out before
they called me to take Brandon and Shamon. It was supposed to be for
two weeks; I've had them now for five years.

It hasn't always been easy. Shamon had nightmares, night after
night. She would wake up screaming. She was seeing monsters. She
would draw pictures of her closet with blood dripping down. Brandon
was on his way to becoming a little thug. He fought in school, and
cursed all the time. He took scissors and cut a teacher's hair. He walked
like a street kid. The first or second week he was here, I told him to clean
his room, and he told me that boys don't do that. Only girls and ladies
clean up. I told him to go to his sister's room, find a dress and put it on,
because he was about to do some cleaning up around here.

He had trouble with his studies, too. He couldn't read a thing, or
write his name when I first got him. He could sing his ABC's but that was

all. I worked with him every day, but he was always in tears. I put him in first grade and it was a nightmare. He wouldn't do his homework and by nine-thirty every night I was ready to choke him and he was ready to choke me. I went to his school and they wanted to put him back in kindergarten. Then I hooked up with Miss Irene, and she started tutoring him.

The relationship between Laws and Hope foster grandparent Irene Bohn, seventy-six, is perhaps the full realization of Brenda Eheart's model of an intergenerational child care community. Laws's dream of providing a stable and permanent home for unwanted children matches perfectly with Bohn's need to remain involved in the lives of children. Bohn grew up as the second of nine children in a staunch Catholic farm family in Tuscola, Illinois, about seventy miles south of Rantoul. At the age of fifteen, she was sent to study to become a nun with the Sisters of St. Francis in Joliet, a southwest suburb of Chicago. Leaving her family and her high school friends was traumatic for Bohn. She did not want to become a nun, but she dared not defy her strict father. "I worried that if I quit and got married, and it turned out to be a bad marriage, I'd never hear the end of it from him," she said.

Under the name Sister Roman ("after my father, whose name was Roman Martin") Bohn became a teaching nun. She served in Catholic schools around the Midwest for two decades. She taught in the affluent Chicago suburbs of Hubbard Woods and Winnetka, and in the inner-city area of Columbus, Ohio, as well as in the impoverished rural community of Benton, Missouri, where classes sometimes started late so that students could pick cotton with their parents. In some schools, she'd have as many as fifty students in one class. She loved teaching and being around young people, although her real dream was to have a family. "I received a good education, and it was a beautiful life, but I always wanted my own children," she said.

Bohn is tall, trim, and meticulously groomed. She playfully describes herself as a "rabble-rouser" and acknowledges that she had to struggle to find contentment as a nun. "I never had the opportunity to be a teenager," she said, "and it was a lonely life in many ways." Two years after celebrating her silver jubilee for twenty-five years in the Franciscan order, she began to experience back and hip pain, ailments she traces to long days spent standing on hard floors in the classroom. Her deteriorating health led to Bohn finally leaving the life that had been chosen for her.

When he learned of her plans to leave the clergy, Bohn's father told her that he'd known for years that she was unhappy, but that he had not wanted to interfere any further in her life. "I can't tell you the tears I shed, but Daddy was beautiful to me when I left the order," Bohn said. "He was worried, though. He feared I wouldn't be able to support myself."

Bohn was forty-five years old when she walked away from the protected life provided by the Sisters of St. Francis. Within a year, she was teaching full-time in a rural school district south of Champaign in central Illinois—and married to a school superintendent.

I hadn't seen much of the world until I married Fred, my gentle giant, and let me tell you, we had a hell of a good time. I call him "my gentle giant" because that's what he was; he was a very good man. He'd been widowed and he had two grown daughters and five grandsons, who are now my stepgrandsons. We had a wonderful thirteen years together, and then he was gone, but he left me with a beautiful stepfamily.

After Fred died, I moved to Crawfordsville, Indiana, where I was a hostess in a retirement home, a grand old mansion that had been willed to the city. I loved it, but I was having trouble with my back again, so I moved to Urbana, nearer to family. I was living alone in a little apartment, doing a lot of walking at the mall and thinking there had to be more to life than this. I came upon a little magazine called *Active Senior*. I was tired when I started to read it, and feeling down. I saw an article about this place called "Hope Meadows." I thought it sounded wonderful, so I called and told them I'd be interested in tutoring children there, and they signed me up in no time.

I do believe that we have the best of both worlds here at Hope Meadows. One morning, I was up early because I'd just lost a brother and I felt like I was all alone in the world. I stepped outside and all of a sudden some child called, "Mornin', Grandma," and I got goosebumps. It made it all worthwhile.

Brandon, Jeanette's adopted boy, was one of my first students when I moved to Hope Meadows. He was a little bitty guy. At first, I didn't think I'd ever reach him. He had never had structure in his life. He had other things on his mind. One day I was really struggling to keep him on track, and he put his hand on my arm and said, "Am I just wasting your time, Grandma?" I told him, "No, that's why I am here, to help you learn."

It took a lot of work to get him to study and focus, but he is a curious child. He had never been exposed to much of the world. We were doing phonics one day and we came upon a picture of a tractor. "What is that?" he asked me. He'd never seen a tractor. So, the next time I went to visit my sister's family on their farm, I took Brandon with me. We were driving there and I could see he was feeling a little nervous. I asked him what was wrong, and he said, "Do they know I'm black?" I said that the color of his skin wouldn't matter. I asked him, "What do you think about me being white?" He answered, "It's okay, Miss Irene."

When we arrived at the farm, my two married nephews picked him right up and put him on a big corn picker and let him ride with them in the cab. His eyes were as big as silver dollars. They said to him, "C'mon, Brandon, we've got work to do." It made me cry to see how they treated him so warmly, and how much he enjoyed it.

My family had never had much contact with African-Americans, but they've grown very attached to Brandon and his family. They've even said that if anything ever happens to me, they want to stay in touch with him and still have him visit. Oh, and you should hear him read now. He couldn't read a word before, but now he does very well for me. He has struggled in school, so I told him that if he earned a star on a paper, I'd give him a quarter. He came over one day with his school bag and pulled out a paper with a star on it. I told him that he deserved a quarter. He reached into the bag and pulled out a handful of papers, put them on the table and said, "See, star, star, star, star, star!" He is a priceless little guy. My heart twangs for these kids.

One night my doorbell rang at quarter 'til seven. It was Brandon. He held out his cupped hand and it was full of wet pennies and a wadded up dollar. "Grandma, may I take you to the movies?" he said. It was my first date in, well, thirteen years. We went to see *Oliver!* And all through the movie, he kept asking if I was comfortable, or if I needed anything. Jeanette told me that she had nothing to do with our "date." It was all his idea.

Irene Bohn's tutoring sessions with Brandon led to her bonding with his sister and with his adoptive mother. Every day after school, Brandon calls "Miss Irene" to see how she is doing. Several times a week, Irene and the Laws family get together for conversation or meals. Irene often cooks a meat loaf or macaroni and cheese in her own kitchen and then brings them over to surprise Jeanette when she comes home from work.

While each senior agrees to volunteer at least six hours a week to assist children or parents, Irene is not "on the clock" for any of this. She considers Jeanette and her children to be family, and the feeling is mutual. The staff at Hope Meadows does not "assign" seniors to families or in any way try to control or guide the formation of relationships between the foster grandparents and families. Their bonds form as they do in most neighborhoods—naturally between individuals who, for whatever reason, relate well to each other. The feelings that form between children and foster grandparents at Hope Meadows are often remarkable and touching, but like the relationships that parents form with the troubled children brought here, they are also laden with risk. Many hearts have been healed at Hope Meadows, but occasionally, some are broken.

In the summer of 1996, Jeanette took Brandon and Shamon with her on a visit to see her family in Providence. While she was there, she received a phone call from Brenda Eheart. "I've got a set of twins coming from DCFS. Nobody can do this but you . . ."

They were high risk, a palm-sized boy and girl born prematurely. They were twelve days old when Jeanette returned from vacation and took custody. Saving "the twins" became a project and a focal point for her, Bohn, and others in the Hope Meadows community over the next eleven months. They were beautiful, tragic children. They could sleep only two hours at a stretch. Miss Irene and Jeanette took shifts. They nursed the children, nourished them to good health, and formed a deep, proprietary love for them.

And then barely a month before the twins' first birthday, an aunt from Chicago notified DCFS that she wanted to take custody of the children. As a relative qualified to parent the children, she had a legitimate claim in the eyes of the court. Jeanette Laws and Miss Irene still get emotional when talking about the day the twins left

Hope Meadows. "When they took those babies out the door, it was like someone ripped my heart out," said Laws.

Added Bohn: "When you set up little bassinets and baby beds and take care of them for eleven months and then they take them away, it is like death. I developed deep, deep feelings for my twinnies, but I learned that you can't allow yourself to bond so closely with the children here. . . ."

Laws and Bohn were heartbroken when the twins were taken away yet they bear no bitterness. The aunt who adopted the babies returns and visits with them regularly. She and her children even stay with Laws so that all of the Hope residents who knew them as infants can renew the bonds. "We have formed a very close relationship," Laws said. "She's like a sister and her family is like mine." When the twins come back, it is something of an event at Hope Meadows. Like many of the children and families who move on, they are still considered a part of the community.

The shared trial of nurturing and then losing the twins brought Irene Bohn and the Laws family even closer together. For all their differences in age, race, and life experiences, the two women are similar in many ways. Both are widowed, highly independent, confident, and devoted to children. With her own family a thousand miles away, Laws has learned to trust and lean on Bohn as her most unlikely "surrogate mother." But the former nun is not the only foster grandparent that she and her children have bonded with. "When I first moved in and before I even had any children, Fran and Bill Biederman were my neighbors. Every day when I'd come home from working in the school, my dinner would be ready. I grew to love them and now, my children do, too," she said. Laws appears to be a favorite of many of her neighbors, too. One spring day, she came home from work to find another older neighbor, Jo Young, planting flowers in Laws's yard.

"There she was on her knees, planting stuff around my birdbath, on her own, just to be nice. Miss Jo also gives Brandon a ride to the school bus stop every morning, and she's always offering to cook dinner for us. She's wonderful. My entire family loves her, too. I think the whole senior component is a wonderful part of Hope Meadows," said Laws. "Without them, it would not be the same here."

I love them, and I've taught my children to love them, because I find that most young people—and the younger they are the worse it gets—are either afraid of older people or they are condescending to them, so I put my children in touch with seniors so they understand that they are people, too. They are just people who have been here longer than they have.

I never knew my grandparents on either side. My children will never know their grandparents, so the seniors here have kind of given them some insight into what grandparents are. Miss Irene is their grandmother, just as the Biedermans and the Youngs are their grandparents, too. They don't care if she is black, blue, pink, or polka dot. Some days she comes in here when I've got nothing left after work and she will start telling them what to do and they say, "Yes, ma'am." There are also times when the babies are having a bad day and she'll sit in the rocking chair and rock them. Then, too, there are times when she'll need to talk about something if she's had a bad day, and I'm there for her. In many ways, she is like my mother.

The Hope Meadows support system is built on familial relationships, and it appears to be working well for Brandon and Shamon. His brash manner has mellowed into a sweet and earnest nature that charms not only his beloved "Miss Irene" but everyone around him. His sister, Shamon, is a budding, lively beauty who now goes to bed at night to dream not of demons, but of becoming an astronaut. She recently attended a NASA Space Camp with her tuition paid by a special fund created for the children of Hope Meadows.

Laws sometimes worries that perhaps this is too good a place. She warns her children that not every elderly white or black person will be glad to hug them; that someday they may live in a neighborhood without playgrounds let alone playground monitors. As someone more accustomed to the urban Northeast, Laws finds Midwestern small-town life and the added comforts of Hope Meadows a bit unsettling sometimes. The Friday night movies with free popcorn at the ICG Center, teen programs on Saturday mornings, and weekend barbecues with people of all ages and colors are all well and good, but she doesn't want her children to be shocked if, one day, they have to live in a less nurturing environment.

Brandon came home one day and some lady had yelled at him on the way home from school. He was shocked! I said, "Welcome to the real world. She yelled at you? Did you survive? You will have to learn to deal with it!" I don't want them to be lulled into a false sense of security. I want them to be able to draw strength from within themselves. I teach them that this is a place of support, but it is not life. I want them to know how to deal with the real deal. Then again, I realize that I could not have four needy children in my care without Hope Meadows or the help of God. I could not house them. I could not clothe or feed them. This place is still evolving and there are still some things it needs to do, but Hope Meadows has made it possible for me to adopt and care for my kids, and I try to always remember that. This is a good place, but it is not the place that makes the difference for the children, it is the people in their lives.

Chapter Three

"It Was a Place for
Seniors, and
Lola Graduated."

On a chilly Tuesday morning in early February, a tiny, elegant, white-haired woman wearing pink-framed eyeglasses, blue jeans, and a creamy cardigan sits serenely in a rocking chair inside the Intergenerational Center at Hope Meadows. Facedown and all but buried in her delicate chest is a very big, black-curled baby girl in pink booties and matching jumper. The infant is asleep and snoring lightly into the Hope grandmother's sweater. "My baby's name is Macy," Lola Myers says quietly. "She lives with my neighbor's family. She was born in mid-September of last year, about the time I came here."

It is Enrichment Day at Hope Meadows, which means parents in the community can drop off their preschoolers and run errands child-free, thanks to senior residents who serve as baby-sitters, story readers, crafts coaches, and playmates. As Myers gently rocks the blissful infant, a raven-haired girl with toffee-toned skin dances up and plants a kiss on the snoozing baby's fat, ripe cheek. "This is her sister, Alyssa. I picked her up after school," Myers says fondly.

Hope Meadows grandparents are not privy to the psychiatric

and medical evaluations, police reports, and legal documents contained in the thick case files and court records that accompany most children from the foster care system. Lola had no way of knowing that the slumbering baby she held was thought to be severely impaired by the drugs her birth mother consumed while pregnant. Nor did she know that the beautiful, beaming girl at her side had been diagnosed with "attachment disorder," which makes it difficult for her to trust or form relationships, particularly with adults. The child's emotional problems are believed to be rooted in the abuse and neglect she suffered at the hands of adults in her earliest years. Because Lola had no knowledge of these children's case histories, she had no expectations for them. The seniors who serve as foster grandparents at Hope Meadows often succeed in reaching the troubled youngsters here simply because they open their hearts to them without qualification.

I had a call to go to the Roberts' house to meet Alyssa's school bus because her mother had to be somewhere else. Alyssa got off the bus and said, "Where's Mom?" and I said, "I don't know, but you are coming home with me today."

"Fine," she told me.

It was like, "So what?" And she came right along. Of course, Bert, my dog, thought I'd brought home a little girl just for him.

It is one of this community's blessings that the healing works both ways. While the children who've been abused or neglected are the primary focus, many of the foster grandparents bring their own complex and poignant histories to Hope Meadows. The seniors accept the children as they come to them, and the young respond in kind.

At eighty years old, Lola Myers has an easy laugh, a sharp wit, and a girlish charm. She is a private woman who doesn't readily give up stories from her life, though she can warm to it, particularly to share her enthusiasm for the Chicago Cubs or sports in general. While she has a "secret" passion for the Charlie Brown comic strip and delights in sending out Snoopy greeting cards to her friends and family, this well-traveled former registered nurse displays an edgier humor, too. During the hoopla over the *Survivor* television show, she noted that she was sick of hearing about it everywhere she turned. "The last time someone mentioned it, I thought, 'Get off it, boys,' " she said.

Alyssa and other children are drawn to Lola because of her childlike size and her gentle but lively manner. Just as she welcomes them with no knowledge of the trials they have endured, the children have no way of knowing that just three years ago, doctors thought Lola would never leave a Florida hospital.

She is barely five feet tall and has never weighed more than one hundred pounds, but at that point her weight had dropped to seventy pounds. "If you can imagine that," said Lola. As a former nurse, Lola knew her condition was dire, and she understood how it had come about. As often happens when one elderly spouse tries to care for another without adequate assistance, Lola had put her own health in jeopardy while trying to attend to the needs of her ailing husband.

My husband's name was Chester, but the family called him "Chick" and that's how I knew him. We met when I was in nurses' training. We weren't supposed to date patients but a girl in my class had treated a guy who'd come in with a burn and then agreed to go out with him. She had a car and he didn't. So it was "Hey, let's all go." I went along and met Chick. He was an ROTC trainer before the war. We got married in September and Pearl Harbor was in December and practically everyone in his unit was sent out of here. He went to Europe in General Patton's Army as an engineer. He built bridges over the Rhine. Then, after the war, he worked in the ROTC program at the University of Illinois where I was a nurse for nonacademic personnel. Later, we moved around: Colorado, Arkansas, North Carolina, Texas. I guess we were pretty restless. We didn't vacation an awful lot. Our idea of vacationing was staying somewhere on a river or on a lake and not doing much of anything. We did like to walk together and our kids and grandkids have inherited that. They all like to hike and to go on trails. Chick and I walked at least two miles every day, and he played golf until he just didn't care about it any longer.

I don't think of those things too much anymore. Chick has been gone over two years, and you go through times when you don't talk about the years you had together. There are times when I just want so badly to talk to him. There are just things you talk about with your spouse and no one else. I miss that. The little things.

We'd been married fifty-six years when he started losing some of his zest for life. He had dementia that came on without too much warning. The doctor said, "I really think we should put him in a nursing home and you can visit him there." I couldn't do that. Neither one of us wanted to be put in a nursing home. I had a bed put in downstairs so I could take care of him and, consequently, I neglected myself. I wasn't eating right. I depleted my electrolytes and my salt. The body has to have salt. I collapsed before he did. They put us both in the hospital, and they didn't think I would live. It was kind of crazy. But I'm a tough old bird. I fooled them all.

I was sick three to four months, from December until March. I had to learn to walk again. So my two daughters—one of them lives in

Rantoul—came down to Florida where we'd been living and as soon as they could they got us out of the hospital. We came up here to a nursing home in Gifford, seven or eight miles from here. Then Chick died two years ago, so I moved to Prairie Village, an assisted living center in Rantoul. It was nice, especially for people who need help with things like meal preparation, but as a friend said, "It was a place for seniors, and Lola graduated."

I was getting a little tired of their type of food. I don't like gravy and it was gravy this and gravy that. And you'd go to lunch or dinner and, I don't mean to be nasty, but all you heard was about illnesses. You name it, they had it. I was a registered nurse so I should be used to that, but it got a little old. I felt it would be nice to be away from it, even though I do miss a few of the people there. I was restless and wanted to be on my own again, and I heard about this place, Hope Meadows, and started checking into it.

When I told the people here I was interested, they had a woman interview me. I said, "Don't you think I'm a little old?" And she said, "No." But I think I'm the oldster of the whole mob here now.

Lola was raised by her grandparents in Odell, Illinois, a farming village of about one thousand residents just ninety miles southwest of Chicago. In her day, it was an even smaller town but one comprised of tightly knit, big families. Her neighbors included an older couple she came to know as "Uncle Spike and Aunt Mart." They were avid Cub fans. "I used to run home after school to catch the end of the baseball games at their house. If the Cubs lost, Aunt Mart would have tears rolling down her face," Lola recalled. She says Hope Meadows is different from her hometown in most ways. It is certainly a busier place, with far more racial diversity. But it is like a rural Midwestern town in that neighbors of all ages take an abiding interest in each other's welfare, and no one is put out to pasture.

You get to this point in life and you think, "Gee, I can still be useful?" Here, you can do as much as you want. Lately they've said I've been putting in a lot of volunteer hours and a few times at night I've been tired, but it's a good tired. It can seem like a long day away from the house, and you do realize why the good Lord gives children to the young. A gal I used to work with said, "I think it's great what you do out there at Hope Meadows, but the volunteer stuff is for you and not for me." Several other people have frowned at me and said I must be a little crazy to be doing this at my age. Maybe I am. But I've always done volunteer work, everywhere we lived. Sometimes it's a little hard for people to understand why you'd want to live in a place like this at this age and not get paid for the work you do, but I'm just old-fashioned in some ways. I think there are things you can do for other people that you don't accept money for.

Some people still think I'm a little crazy, but I'm "me" enough that I was willing to give this place a try for a while, and I think I like it. There are a lot of caring people here. That's one thing that is really interesting to me and makes me feel good. The Calhoun family lives across the street. They are a big, big family. They have seven or eight adopted kids now, but the mother, Debbie, is always calling me and asking if I need anything from the store or if I need one of the kids to walk the dog. And I'm supposed to be the one helping her with her little ones! They are really caring people, and I love their boy Marty. He is always dying to take Bert for a walk.

I've had a lot of cute things happen with the kids here. One afternoon I was working in the library from four to six P.M. and a little girl came up for reading time. She looked at me and said, "Are you going to die?"

I said, "Yes, someday, and you will someday, too."

She looked at me like she didn't believe it. So I said, "That is part of God's plan." She seemed to accept that but she started studying my arms and then she rubbed on them and asked, "Why are your arms like that?" I told her that as you get older, your skin gets thinner and your veins show more. I told her that she has veins under the skin too but they don't show because she is still young.

She took all this in and then finally asked if she could sit on my lap. We read not one, but two books that day. You know, that was the only child ever to ask me if I was going to die. I must have looked just wretched that day.

On another day, another little girl asked to see my teeth. I showed them to her and she said, "Do you have your own teeth?" I said that I did and she said, "They are really white." Lord, you never know what they are going to ask you.

I look at some of these children, and I think how fortunate they are to have this place because when their families broke up they probably didn't have what I had. My grandparents were so loving. I was really fortunate to have them. No one can entertain kids twenty-four hours a day, but here they have people who enjoy them and love them and give them a sense of security and I'm sure that's important.

Kids have to know they are being cared for. They have to know love. I think they respect some discipline, although they'd never put that into words, and security too. Time is probably the most precious element we have, and that may be why the kids here seem so happy. People at Hope Meadows have time for them.

Chapter Four

"HIS CARING CAME THROUGH."

Larry Gardner arrived at Hope Meadows as a fifty-two-year-old foster child. He was married, with grown children, but he carried into adulthood the wounded psyche of a boy taken from an abusive parent and shuttled from foster home to foster home like furniture that didn't match. In 1995, Gardner moved into Hope Meadows with his wife, Beverly, hoping to help other uprooted children heal from similar histories. Gardner understood their alienation and disorientation. He knew what it was like to feel disconnected from the rest of the world and roughed up by it for no good reason. His parents had never married. His mother was unable to care for him because of her own difficulties. He spent his rootless childhood in transit within the child welfare system. "What saved him, really, was that he was able to move in with his grandmother and stepgrandfather for his last two years of high school, and that put him on the right road," said Bev Gardner.

To meet Larry Gardner and to know him casually, you'd never sense that he'd had a troubled moment in his life, his friends and family said. There was no anger. He didn't drink, or smoke. This was a steady-going, family man with an easy smile, who worked for the city of Rantoul's water and sewer department for thirty-two years. "The only time I saw his past come through was around Christmas. Every year he'd get kind of quiet around that time," Bev said. "He told me that's when he was taken from his mother, and he was removed from foster homes several times then, too, so it made him sad."

Bev and Larry came to Hope Meadows at the urging of their friends Debbie and Kenny Calhoun, who moved in just a few months before them. In most cases, it is the women who are engaged by Hope's mission, and though Bev Gardner is a caring and compassionate person, in this case it was her husband who was most drawn to Brenda Eheart's goal of rebuilding the lives of neglected children. Larry Gardner identified with the youngsters and their empty hearts, said Bev.

His caring came through. He was a magnet for the kids at Hope. They'd come up to him and tell him that their mother drank all the time and that her boyfriends used drugs and were mean to them, and he'd say that he knew exactly how they felt because he'd gone through the same things. He told them he understood, and that meant everything. It wasn't unusual to see him playing baseball with fifteen to twenty kids, or running up the basketball court with them. He told me that once a kid found out he'd been a foster child, too, they just trusted him. Once a boy came up to him and out of the blue said, "I miss my mom but I don't want to be with her because of what happened." Larry told him that he still missed his mom, too.

I became a foster parent because of what my husband had gone through. I'd had my own children, but they were all in their thirties, grown up and moved to Massachusetts and South Carolina. Because of what Larry had experienced, I wanted to make a home for kids who had problems and could not be with their parents. I wanted to do something so kids wouldn't have to go from home to home like he did. I wanted to make a good, nurturing home for them.

The middle-aged couple had hardly unpacked in their six-bedroom Hope Meadows home before they were asked to serve as temporary guardians for three young siblings who stayed with them three months and then were returned to their birth mother. On their heels came the Gardners' first permanent placement, an abandoned infant whose plight had made the national news. Jacob arrived in November of 1995. He was three and a half months old, but already had a wrenching history. As a newborn, he was found on the floor in a restroom at Little Company of Mary Hospital in Evergreen Park, a blue-collar suburb of Chicago. Doctors suspected that the unknown mother was a drug user, so they immediately placed the infant on a respiratory monitor. Unfortunately, that marked the innocent child as a potential burden for anyone who took him in. It didn't help that the story of his abandonment was covered in the media. No agency or foster parent wanted to take on a difficult child with the media watching.

Because of his suspect health, Jacob was first sent as an emergency placement to St. Coletta's of Illinois, a well-regarded Catholic home for special needs children in Palos Park, a Chicago suburb. He remained there for three months while a caseworker for the State Department of Children and Family Services tried to find a foster home or child care agency to take him. Eighteen agencies turned him down. Again, no one wanted another child from an uncertain background with possible long-term health problems. Because of the mounting costs of keeping Jacob in St. Coletta's, the DCFS caseworker was about to put him in an emergency foster home. But a St.

Coletta's social worker, who had heard about Hope Meadows from a coworker, made a call. She was told that Hope Meadows was created for just this type of child. And so Larry and Bev Gardner welcomed the first of their new family.

Jacob had been very well taken care of at St. Coletta's. And he was not sick at all, so they must have been wrong about him being a crack baby. He was just a beautiful baby and he's a beautiful child, now four years old, and while he's noticed the racial difference, he's never asked why he's black and I'm white. He considers me his natural mother.

Jacob came to us in November of 1995. Next came a second boy in December. He was an adolescent with a teenager's rebellious nature. In the end, he did not stay. He is still in the foster care system outside of Hope Meadows. Then on January 16, 1996, came our two girls, who are sisters; Rachel, who is now eight, and Becky, who is thirteen. It was really hectic at first because we had kids from different families and races—they were Hispanic, Caucasian, and African-American—coming out of different environments. They all had problems, except for Jacob, who was the best baby and best child I'd ever had.

The three oldest children immediately exhibited serious problems. Still, the Gardners were committed to helping them, and to giving them and Baby Jacob a permanent home. The adolescent boy came from a large and turbulent family. His mother had reported that she'd become pregnant with him after being gang-raped at the age of sixteen. He'd lived in nine foster homes by the time he came to Hope Meadows. He was sensitive, intelligent, protective of his siblings in foster care, and also rebellious, given to running away, and streetwise. Bev said that Larry Gardner worked hard to form a bond with him and, for a time, appeared to be having a positive effect.

The two blond sisters were brought to the Gardners after having been in and out of thirteen foster homes. Their birth mother once
kidnapped them from a foster home and took them out of state to
avoid losing them again. "They came from awful circumstances,"
Bev said. They had two half-sisters, who were also taken from the
mother, who had been involved with the child welfare system since
the age of six. Caseworkers reported that the mother was known to
leave her children alone with no food. They showed symptoms of
physical, sexual, and emotional abuse. According to Bev, the
mother, who had an extensive criminal record, had once become
enraged at Rachel and Becky and tried to run them over with her car.

She and Larry spent hours working to win the children's trust,
to ease their fears and suspicions, to teach them that not all adults
were predators or victimizers.

We talked to them a lot. We wouldn't ask questions other than to
ask if they were having a good or bad day. If they wanted to talk and
share, we'd listen to them. Larry and I thought that was real important.
We also kept them in counseling, and I stayed home full-time and
worked with the counselors. I couldn't have handled their problems and
worked, too. There was no way. We really felt we were getting their
problems under control after two years of hard work. We were prepared
to adopt them all. The courts had terminated all of the parental rights. In
fact, we had a court date for Jacob's adoption, but then one night, I woke
up, and heard Larry breathing erratically . . .

We went to bed at twelve o'clock and I woke up about two. I heard
this noise. I was foggy at first because I was trying to get awake. I heard
this sound; it was almost like snoring, and I said, "Larry, roll over, you're
snoring." And he didn't roll over. I started to go back to sleep, but then it
hit me. *He isn't snoring, he's gasping for air.* So I jumped up and I turned

on the lights as he rolled over on his back. He couldn't talk to me. He couldn't move his body or anything. And all he did was lay there and just gasp for air like he was taking real big breaths, one right after the other. So I ran over and I grabbed the phone and called 911, then I called Al Pena, a senior neighbor, and I told him that Larry was having trouble breathing. Mr. Pena used to work as a medic when he was in the service, and so he said he'd get his stethoscope and get dressed and be right over. By the time he got there, Larry had no vital signs whatsoever. He was already starting to turn cold. I couldn't get him to wake up. I couldn't get him to do anything. When Al came over, he couldn't either. We both tried to do CPR on him and sometime during this our oldest foster son came into our bedroom and asked if Larry was going to be okay. I told him yes, and to go back into his room. I did not want him to see what was happening. First the police came. Then two ambulances came. The medics put Larry on the floor and started to work on him. They had to use those paddles on him. They would start to bring him back and then his heart would fade back out again. And I knew he was dead. They continued to work on him for about a half-hour. One of the officers told me, "Bev, you'd better get someone here to spend time with you, because it does not look good."

I said, "I know."

Hope parent Debbie Calhoun came running down the street in her pajamas, assessed the drama playing out under the glare of red and white emergency lights, and returned home to dress for a long campaign of consoling and mourning. Hope senior Al Pena, the former military man who'd served on the Chanute base, stood watch over the four children who had come to love and depend on Larry Gardner as their father and protector. Al didn't tell them anything. He figured that if the worst happened, they would know soon enough. Another Hope parent, Joyce Hill, who has since moved away, accompanied Deb Calhoun as she drove Bev Gardner to the hospital.

We went on down to the emergency room and they escorted us into this private room and I thought, "Well, this is really it." I already knew. A doctor came and said that Larry had a severe, massive heart attack, and that he went right away. I burst into tears and everybody started crying. Then after a little while, they let me go in and spend time with Larry. I just stood there looking at him and thinking how much he loved the kids. He died on the thirtieth. We were going to adopt Jacob on the third. Instead, that was the day we buried Larry. So that was really hard. I asked Debbie, "Do you think my kids are going to be taken from me?" That was one of the first things I thought about right there at the hospital. Because I'd lost him, I felt like I might lose the kids as well.

The night of Larry Gardner's death and the events that followed are often cited among Hope Meadows residents as a sort of cornerstone event in the formative years of their neighborhood. Many say the tragic death of one of their most dedicated and well-liked neighbors brought them together as a true community. Lasting bonds were formed as neighbors who'd been strangers outside this five-block area came together, wept, grieved, and slowly mended.

While Bev talked with doctors and took care of matters at the hospital, her neighbors dressed and fed the unknowing children and sent them to school, telling them only that Larry had become sick in the night and had to go to the hospital. When Larry's death was confirmed, the same Hope Meadows neighbors went to the school and took the children from their classrooms. One of the boys said it should have been him that died instead of Larry. Another asked to go to his foster father's room. There, he tenderly touched his clothing. Then he went through Larry's toolbox, touching each tool, trying to reclaim some of what he'd lost that day.

Throughout the morning and on through the grieving and memorials that followed neighbors stood watch, cooked meals, ran errands, helped and consoled Bev Gardner and the four young people who'd lost the first dedicated father they'd ever known. "It seemed like it went on for a long time," Bev recalled. Hope Meadows was created as a healing place, but it can scar as easily as any other neighborhood struck by tragedy. Larry Gardner's death was a communal experience that bonded its residents, but it also served as a reality check: Even this dedicated place is not protected from emotional upheaval and sabotaged dreams. It was a draining experience for all, but the people of the community responded with genuine compassion.

My family came for the services, and they said they'd never seen a community pull together like ours did when someone passed away. Debbie Calhoun even went with me to pick out a casket. She helped me take care of the business. She and the other neighbors later had a plaque made and they held a service for Larry and people talked about him. The funeral itself was packed. Standing room only. Brenda Eheart gave a eulogy and read this letter that Becky had written to her a few weeks earlier:

Dear Brenda. These are the reasons I like being in Bev's and Larry's house. First of all, they take us out to Sirloin Stockade. And they care for us. They are the best mom and dad in the entire Universe. They take the time to talk to me about my feelings. Nobody ever took the time for that. They let us go on long rides, walks, picnics, hikes, and trips. They take care of our clothes and hair. This is the best home I ever been in. Bev is my mom! Larry and Bev not only take good care of me, but the others in my home. Brenda, you are special too for choosing us to come to Hope Meadows and live in Bev and Larry's house. I will never forget this for the rest of my life.

The counselors at Hope Meadows worked with the Gardners' foster children during the grieving process. They warned Bev that in the aftermath of Larry's death she was probably going to have rough going with the three oldest. These were children who'd finally found some permanence and stability in their fractured lives, and now they'd been robbed of it. Faced with more uncertainty, and fearing another rejection, the youngsters were bound to act out in anguish and anger, their counselors warned. And they did. "You don't know how many times I was going to throw in the towel," Bev Gardner said.

Bev didn't know if she could handle the challenges. At one point, her frustration was so great that she called the DCFS caseworker still assigned to her daughters and demanded that they be removed from her house. The caseworker talked her down from her anger that time. But in another instance, Bev felt she had no choice but to surrender. At the height of her grieving and despair over Larry's death, Bev began to suspect that the oldest boy in their home had betrayed her trust for reasons that must remain confidential. It was true to his history as a severely abused and neglected child, but it shocked her and frightened her, and she decided that it was impossible for him to remain under her care.

Bev thought Larry had reached this boy, but when allegations arose, she felt she could no longer trust him. She demanded that he be taken from her home. Some within Hope encouraged her not to give up on the boy. She felt that she was not giving up on him so much as protecting herself and the other children. A few neighbors sided with her. Others did not understand. The community that had come together so quickly in tragedy began to pull apart in controversy.

Bev was torn. She questioned whether she was fit to parent such children at all. She had serious doubts about going through with her plans to adopt Jacob and the two girls.

It was a horrible time for me. I finally just took off. I went on a cruise. I had to get away to make a decision about what I wanted to do with my life, and with their lives, too. I met a woman, an author, who was wonderful. She helped me find ways to make my own decisions. Then I came back, still torn, and talked to a Hope counselor who helped me see that these children had lost their father, but they still needed their mother. I decided to go ahead and adopt Jacob, Rachel, and Becky. I did it, but after a while, I realized that I could no longer live in the house where Larry had died. There were just too many memories. I looked at other houses within Hope, but I finally decided that I needed to get out of the neighborhood, too. We are still a part of Hope. We still visit and attend activities there, but now we live on the other side of town, in our own house. And we are thriving, all of us.

My kids think of Hope as the place where they went to find a good home and get adopted. They still feel connected to it in a positive way, and so do I. There are a lot of things about living there that are hard. But I think that comes with the territory, doesn't it?

Becky, the older of the two sisters, was Bev's most difficult foster child after the oldest boy was removed. But once Bev adopted the three children, Becky's behavior changed dramatically. The removal of uncertainty in her life seemed to transform her from a quarrelsome, defiant child to one who expressed gratitude at the opportunity for a normal life. At thirteen, Becky is very much aware of her good fortune in being adopted and given a home. She has undergone intensive therapy and counseling because of the abuse she experienced before coming to Hope Meadows, so some of the things she says sound as though they are crafted for adult ears. But her behavior bears out her words. She is doing well in school, socially and otherwise, and she and Bev, who has remarried, have formed a close bond. When she appeared on the *Oprah* show's segment about Hope Meadows, Becky told her interviewer, "Hope Meadows saved my life."

I came here and met my mom, who has really been an inspiration in my life. I would probably be at the corner of junior high smoking dope and shooting drugs in my veins if it wasn't for her. I would probably be a prostitute today if not for her. My birth mother was leading me in the wrong directions. She was not showing me the right way. My mother now is showing me the road to success.

Hope Meadows has provided me with a nurturing place. Everyone cares about you there. The seniors are like a second set of grandmothers and grandfathers. It's not like you are the odd man out anymore. Most of the kids are just like you, and they can relate to some of your problems. At Hope, I felt like part of a family and a community because my mom had so many friends who brought me into their families, too. When her husband, Larry, died, she could have left without us. She could be in a condo in Florida now. She had the option. But she loved us so much that she stayed.

I was just turning seven when we came to Hope. We drove up and Larry said come on in, and he and my mom made us very comfortable and helped us unpack and rearrange the bedroom the way we wanted it. I wasn't used to being treated like that. We slept on boards at our own house when we were little. At our first dinner with Bev and Larry, they asked me how many hot dogs I wanted. I was like, "I have a choice?" I usually only got half of a hot dog because we were so poor. I still remember that first dinner with them. We had hot dogs and beans and barbecue and onions and we liked them.

Before we went to bed that first night, Larry and my mom asked if we were comfortable, and then she read us a story before we went to bed. I'd never had that happen. And we had our own bathroom we could decorate any way we wanted. We were in seventh heaven. It was so much better than what I'd had before. I was like the Cinderella of my own family. I had to clean the toilets with my bare hands. I had all the responsibility for all four kids living with us. I didn't realize how bad it was until I came to Hope Meadows and experienced luxury.

Once streetwise, Becky is now therapywise. She can name each of the counselors, psychologists, and psychiatrists she has seen over the years—about a half-dozen of them. She says that none of their methods matches what she found in a permanent home with a dedicated parent, and in a community that she knows is there to support her.

I think all the counselors haven't helped me as much as my mom has. They always wanted me to go back and back and talk about what had happened to me, but it didn't seem like they helped me with my future. They said if I didn't let it out, it would stay bottled up inside me, but I have probably let out my past three hundred times. I don't think it's going to explode anymore.

I remember, painfully, living with my birth mother. She got mad at me in a hotel once and picked me up by the arms and threw me against the bed and a screw in the bed went into my leg. She locked me in the bathroom and told me to sit there and bleed to death. I was three or four. She would starve me. She would starve all of us. This really bothers me: My great-grandmother left me a china cabinet with all kinds of stuff in it, and my birth mother kept her dope and her drugs in there. It was left to me but she kept it and did stuff with it. I didn't feel good about myself. I wasn't very happy with myself. I couldn't love myself and I couldn't care about my grades. I felt that I was the only one going through these problems and that it wasn't okay to go through this sort of stuff, and that I was weird or unusual.

I was in thirteen foster homes and that's probably not good to do, skipping from house to house. No one really loves you. You think, "They are just going to give me up again. I'm not good enough for them."

After Larry Gardner's death, Becky felt "the odds were very high" that she and her sister would once again be sent to another foster home. "It would be unusual for a foster parent who had her husband die to keep kids who were not her biological kids," she thought then.

But she kept us, and she and I are so much alike now. We say the same things and think the same things. Me and my mom can sit here and cry at a movie or talk about stuff and cry. She will cradle me even though I'm a hundred and some pounds, and might break her knee. But I don't feel like I'm fat anymore, even though I may be. I don't feel fat. Now, I feel very high on myself. I feel beautiful. I care about my grades. I'm on the honor roll and I'm going to run for president, or maybe vice president of the student council.

Tomorrow is career day at school, and I don't know what I want to do for sure. I want to be a foster mom, or a doctor because I want to help people—because people have helped me. I want to make a difference in their lives and lead kids off the wrong path onto the right path. I think I lost part of my childhood, but I'm gaining it back right now.

Chapter Five

"I DON'T FEEL LIKE
I HAD A CHILDHOOD."

Bertie Levitt describes herself as "five foot one and three-fourths" with curly, permed hair "dyed the color of a new penny." Though she is sixty-one years old, Bertie is quite proud of her standing on the Hope Meadows basketball court, where she serves as a monitor and occasionally subs as point guard. "Grandma Bertie" still has her hesitation dribble, as well as a tomboy's swagger that belies both the travails of her life and the deep well of her empathy for the children here. None of these boys and girls rescued from abusive and neglectful homes have to tell Bertie how much they've hurt. How angry they've been. How unloved they've felt. She knows to reach out to them even before they signal a need. "A lot of the kids come in and, at first, they don't want to be hugged," she says. "I'll tell them that I want a hug anyway, and sometimes I get it. There are a few, though, that I'm still working on."

Bertie is a veteran of the battlegrounds that produced these shell-shocked children. Her life has been a struggle against hurts inflicted in childhood. She became a ward of the state at age nine, and lived in a children's home until she turned seventeen. She never felt loved. She never felt like she belonged. She sees herself in every Hope child. And in this community designed to restore lost childhoods, she sees hope for their salvation from the hardscrabble life that was her fate.

"I don't feel like I had a childhood," she said. And so, she has come to Hope Meadows to prevent others from losing theirs. In the process, Bertie has found a sense of belonging that she'd never known before.

My dad and mom were fifteen years old when they got married. My mom got pregnant and Grandpa made my dad marry her. We mostly lived with my grandparents. I don't remember living with my parents except for the drinking and being beat with a razor strap by my dad. He did it when he was drunk and didn't like what was on the table. He'd throw the food up against the wall. I'd always thought that my parents just didn't want us. I found out many years later that the court took us away. My dad had another woman so my mom divorced him. I found out from a paper that my aunt had saved, a divorce paper, that my dad would not support us and my mother was so young they didn't think she could take care of us so they took us and put us in the custody of the court. They sent us to the Cunningham Children's Home in Urbana. My older brother was ten. I was nine. My sister was eight, and we had a little baby brother who wasn't even two.

The boys went to the men's dormitory and my sister and I slept in the women's dorm. I had nice long hair when I went in, but they strapped me to a chair and cut it. It was brown, long, and pretty and I didn't want them to cut it so I was fighting with them and fussing. I wouldn't stab anybody, but I was rebellious and ornery.

As I grew up, I felt unwanted and unloved. I felt rejected. I never saw my dad after we were taken away. My mother would send money for us and we would get to go see her so I didn't feel as rejected by her as by Dad. All the years we lived in the children's home I never saw him. He was raising his new family. My mother got married again when I was thirteen. We got to go to their house maybe once a month.

We didn't get attention and love at the children's home; we got discipline, schooling, and food. We worked every night after school. When I was nine years old, I had to do the washing. I'd almost lose myself inside those big dryers. When I got older, we had to iron everybody's clothes and help cook and we'd have to set the table the right way, and we always dusted our own furniture and the stairways, and made our own beds. The bell would ring to get us up in the morning and it would ring again signaling us to line up after washing. Then we'd march to the cafeteria when there was another bell. They'd order us to sit down at big round tables and order us to go here and there. We never got hugged.

We had one or two housemothers who were old maids. They would pull our ears and dig fingernails into our arms and draw blood and drag us around. They were just contrary old women. Those old maids who took care of us were really something else. They were always running us down. I was on the toilet one time and one of them said, "You sound like an old cow in there." I was only nine or ten years old. They were always picking on us. The guys got by with everything but the girls got beat up and spanked.

We weren't allowed off the property except with adults or on the bus. We rode to school on a children's home bus. I felt like an outsider because the kids at school called us "little orphans" and treated us like we weren't anything because we couldn't do any activities. We had to come back to the home and do cooking and ironing and cleaning after school. We didn't get to do any extra activities like the other kids. I like music and I wouldn't have minded being in a music club or on the student body. I would have liked to have been outdoors more. I loved sports and I would have liked to have been on one of the teams. I was a sports nut more than anything else. I climbed trees and played baseball and football and rode bikes. We didn't have TV until Gene Autry, the cowboy star, came to the children's home and gave us a television set for each dormitory. I was in high school and it was the first time I saw one.

When I was fourteen, we got a new couple at the children's home: Carroll and Maude Guard. We called them Mom and Pop. He was a deputy sheriff and they were from the small town of Homer. They were precious. They were the most loving parents I ever had. They treated us like family and they would take us to fun places like Turkey Run in their station wagon. And if we had personal problems, Mom would say, "Come and talk to me." It was more personal. I never had a father until Pop Guard. When you are raised in a children's home, you don't feel that personal contact. The Guards really made sure we felt love.

Bertie likes to show off a wide scar that twists angrily around her lower right arm. She tells the story of how she got it when she was three years old, living with her grandparents, and helping her grandmother do laundry. Bertie was feeding clothing into the washing machine's mechanical wringer when it grabbed her arm and yanked it through. The machine had to be taken apart to free her mangled arm. The symbolism of the scar is not lost on her. "I been through the wringer all my life," she says with a rueful cackle.

At the age of seventeen, Bertie left the Cunningham Children's Home and moved in with her mother, but her stepfather "wouldn't leave his hands off me and my sister or my girlfriends." The lack of loving, supportive relationships in her childhood left Bertie wounded and vulnerable to predators and abusers. She married disastrously and often. "I was always trying to buy love." She was not quite eighteen when she married for the first time and headed down an even rougher road than she'd already known.

My girlfriend and my sister and I met these Air Force guys in an Urbana restaurant and they took us to the taverns in Danville. They didn't like that we sat in the backseat and wouldn't play their games on the way, so they left us. We were walking along the highway back to Urbana in the rain when this guy and his buddy drove by, turned around, and came back to offer us a ride. The guy driving liked my girl-friend. His friend took a shine to me. I was seventeen and a half when I married him.

When he was cold sober my first husband was the best man alive, but when he was drunk he was absolutely crazy. I was his doormat. I took care of him and cleaned him up and he'd go out with other women while I worked and ironed and cooked. He ran around with every woman he could find. I became bitter and built a wall around myself.

I'd always wanted kids, and when I was growing up I wanted a husband of my own and a home of my own and kids of my own. But I had very bad luck with men. After my first divorce, I met an old boyfriend and we got reunited. He was an alcoholic, too, and ended up moving in with me for three years. He had kids he would not take care of. He'd be drunk and not remember where he'd taken them. Finally, I said, "Me or the booze, take your choice." He took the booze, so I kicked him out.

In spite of her tumultuous personal life, Bertie worked for thirty years as a nursing assistant at Carle Foundation Hospital, a large regional hospital in Champaign, about twenty miles south of Rantoul. She did tours in general surgery, orthopedics, urology, "everywhere they needed me." Her second marriage was to one of the hospital's security guards. It quickly became apparent that his ex-wife was still in the picture. Bertie bailed out after three months.

I let him go and it hit me like a ton of bricks. I built up more bitterness. I came to think that I was only good for one thing, having sex with men. I started going out with anybody and everybody. I don't remember most of them. I dated a cop and moved in with him, but I went home one night and no one was there. He'd gone back to his ex-wife. Then I started dating a guy in prison. Oh, Lord! I had the run of the mills, I tell you! He was on work release when I met him and I felt sorry for him. He started drinking a lot and went uptown and stole some liquor, and got in trouble. Because he was on work release he got sent back to prison for another year.

He was in the Pontiac penitentiary first. I visited him there, and then he got transferred down south to Vandalia and I drove there every week, faithfully, for a year. When the year was up, they parolled him to me. I didn't want him to live with me but that was a condition of his parole. I got him a job. I worked third shift at the hospital and he drank while I worked. He had an affair with a barmaid and walked out on me. That was it. Bye-bye, baby.

That was the last time I loved somebody that much. He later had a heart attack and died in prison when he was fifty. Something did come out of our relationship, though. After I became a Christian, he came back to see me. He thought I might sleep with him but I told him I didn't do things like that anymore. I took him to my pastor and my pastor prayed for him and I told him to thank Jesus for coming into his heart. He called me two days later and said he was on the run from an armed robbery. He asked me to take him to jail to give up. That was the last time I saw him, in the sheriff's office. He wasn't good to me, but it still hurt to take him into jail.

When her stormy life found an unusual calm a few years ago, Bertie began having haunted dreams of headless men—men she'd loved but couldn't trust. Such men passed through Bertie's life like stabbing pains. Even when she'd made peace with the first who'd hurt and abandoned her—her father—he was taken away.

I was working in Danville one day and they told me somebody is outside to see you. It was my father. I don't know if he was half-drunk or half-sober. He asked me to forgive him for what he did not do for me. I wasn't a Christian at that point, but I forgave him because by then I understood where he was coming from. My parents were forced to get married at fifteen. It was 1939, during the Depression. It was a hard life. I said I forgave him and I still loved him, and we got real close for a while. One day on the television they said a whole family died of carbon monoxide poisoning in their trailer. They went to sleep and never woke up. It was my dad and his second wife and their nine-year-old and five-year-old. Dad was only forty-one. Just when we were getting real close.

In 1980, Bertie "gave up men and liquor and became a Christian." A coworker at the hospital told her she needed to change her life and focus on making her peace with God. She joined a Bible home study group that became her surrogate family. Within it, she found the first man who treated her with respect and affection. She was forty-five years old.

He was a maintenance man for the Knights of Columbus Hall, a jack-of-all-trades. Glen treated me like a queen. Anything I wanted to do or anyplace I wanted to go was all right with him. At first it was a little rough because there was a bit of a wall built around me. I told him that I'd taken care of myself all my life and I didn't need a man to take care of me, now. I told him he couldn't come around me if he'd been drinking or if he acted like he was going to hit me. I'd been hurt. He'd been hurt, too. We went to counseling for three months with a preacher and we worked out our problems. We were married five and a half years. We had a house in a little town and we were going to buy four acres in the woods. But then he died of cancer.

After Glen died, I told the Lord I didn't want to have nothing to do with nobody. I got fond of a couple guys but I wouldn't play their games. I wanted a Christian. I figure if a man loves Jesus the way he should, he would love me right. Now, I leave it up to the Lord. I've lived alone so long I've gotten used to it. I do get lonely. I do worry that if I fall how will anybody know I'm hurt. But I have my neighbors and the children here, and my Bible home study group. Those people are so precious to me. For my birthday last year they gave me presents and cards and balloons and stuff. I have never had that done for me in my life.

Bertie came to Hope Meadows to escape violence in the apartment complex she'd moved to after Glen's death. She'd confided her fears about drug dealers and shootings to a fellow congregation member at the Christian Life Church. The friend was Carolyn Casteel, the administrator at Hope Meadows. Carolyn encouraged Bertie to apply for the community's foster grandparents program. She moved into one of the three-bedroom senior apartments among the family residences. She lives there with her two dogs, PK and Candy, among scores of children who need just what Bertie needed, but never received.

When kids first get here, I can see they are rebellious. They hold stuff inside. They don't want anyone to touch them and reach inside them. They hide their feelings. You know when not to touch them by the look in their eyes. I've seen it in a lot of kids who don't know how to show affection. They don't want to be touched. They are scared. But eventually they come out of that, and then they look so peaceful. They smile more after they have been here a while. They get a lot of love and attention here. They have more of a family setting, with parents and brothers and sisters living with them. If me and my brothers and sisters had been sent here, we would have been more of a family. There is more love with sisters and brothers.

It is a Tuesday morning at Hope Meadows and, amid small groups of children at play, and seniors in conversation inside the Intergenerational Center, Bertie has staked claim to a blond, coverall-button-bursting, sixteen-month-old who is cooing ardently at her from his high chair. She looks away from him only to dispense hugs to the other children who come to her in a wobble-legged parade. "I never did have kids and I don't know why I love the little things so much now, but I do," she says. Like many of Hope's foster grandparents, Bertie does far more for the children and their parents than is required. Each schoolday, her 1989 Chevrolet Celebrity station wagon marks up another few miles onto its overachieving odometer (139,000 at last count) as Bertie drives to pick up Keri Roberts, nine years old and a third-grader at Broadmeadow Elementary. Keri's mother, Michelle, has six children, including a three-year-old and an infant, both of whom nap at midafternoon. So Bertie gladly drives her neighbor's daughter home from school each day. Keri was so withdrawn and unresponsive when she was brought to Hope Meadows six years ago, her adoptive mother feared she might be autistic. Under Michelle's care and in this nurturing environment, the girl has blossomed into an avid reader, honor student, and highly animated chatterbox. She showers Grandma Bertie with homemade cards and gifts. "Her cards are better than you can get in a Hallmark store," Bertie proudly noted.

If the children brought here could be poured into a pitcher, Bertie would drink them down in deep gulps. She is so eager to give them what she needed, to save them from what befell her. Few people have been as unlucky in love or life as Bertie Levitt. Few are so lucky, or so grateful to have found a place where one person's needs serve as another's salvation.

Chapter Six

"I Am Insane, Really."

"What do abused and neglected children need?" Hope Meadows
founder Brenda Eheart was asked.

*"Linda and Tory Hines and whatever it is that they have. If I
could bottle it, the world would be a far better place,"* she replied.

Huge boxes of crackers, cookies, cereal, and other family staples
line the dining room wall in the Hope Meadows home of Linda and Tory
Hines. Food and household supplies bought in bulk are common com-
modities in a neighborhood where families are large, budgets are tight,
and economies of scale carefully applied. Crises large and small are
also part of everyday life at Hope Meadows. When the telephone rings
at midday, Linda calmly reaches for it, patiently listens to a briefing
from the exasperated teacher of her adopted seven-year-old daughter,
and then without raising her voice or even hardening her tone, she
talks the troubled child down from yet another emotional eruption.

Why are you throwing a tantrum, Ashley?

Are you supposed to have chocolate milk? Well then, it shouldn't
be an issue with the teacher, should it?

Why does it matter to you that someone had to sit at another table?

But you refused to come to the classroom to eat. You threw yourself down and wouldn't walk when she asked you to go.

So, you lost ten minutes of recess. Now, you'll sit there quietly so you can play the rest of your recess time. Right?

And, the rest of the day is going to go how?

Good, because I don't want any more complaints. I want to see plusses on your sheet today.

Okay, now put Miss Metzger back on the phone.

Many children and many family crises ago, Linda and Tory Hines met in an Urbana, Illinois, elementary school. They quickly became boyfriend and girlfriend, chasing each other around the playground nearly every day, until Linda's family moved to Detroit, abruptly ending the relationship. Four years later, her family moved back, and Linda rejoined Tory in high school. Their relationship rekindled. Linda and Tory are both upbeat and down-to-earth. Both came from large, extended families. They shared a love of family and when they talked of the future back in high school they agreed that they wanted a lot of children around. They got their wish more quickly than they'd dreamed. After graduation, they married and Tory took a job in a day care center. Linda enrolled in a community college and worked part-time in an Olan Mills portrait studio. She'd only been there a short time when she began to notice that her customers included one big family after another—all from a place in Rantoul called Hope Meadows.

"We're here for our adoption pictures," they told her. When they described Hope Meadows and its purpose to Linda, she could hardly contain herself. "I talked to a lady who said they are looking for more parents to adopt and that they have housing with lots of space for kids, and I said, "Oh, my God, let me call my husband!" We called Hope Meadows that day and set up an appointment, and lo and behold, we got accepted!

There was concern at first among the staff at Hope Meadows about my age. But then they interviewed me and they got over it. I was only twenty-two when we moved here. I'm twenty-five now, and Tory is twenty-eight. Since we've moved here, he got a job at a youth detention center on the other side of the old base. And I'm a full-time stay-at-home mom, thanks to Hope Meadows.

I had been trying to become a foster mother since I was eighteen. My godmother had been a foster parent for years, so I had (foster) god-sisters in the system who would come to my godmother and then go back to their birth parents, or to another foster home. That devastated me. One of her foster kids was five and the other was four. I was eight.

I didn't know their full stories, only that their own mom wouldn't take care of them. My godmother had them for four years and then they went back to their mom. After a year, their birth mother abandoned them at a gas station in the dead of winter. They were then sent some-where else, because the state said my godmother had gotten too attached to them. She'd had them for four years! You can darn well believe she got attached to them! That experience hurt us. We still talk about them all the time, wondering where they are and what they look like. We never had contact with them again, though I heard they were somewhere in Iowa.

I used to take my little godsisters skating in Champaign all the time. There is a box at the skating place that you can put names into and win a free birthday party. I still put their names in it when I take my own kids there, even though I haven't seen them since we were all little girls.

Ever since my godsisters left, I've wanted to make a difference in the lives of foster children. Tory worked in day care for five years and he loves kids, too. We are kid crazy. Tory comes from a family of six. My two sisters and one brother and I were raised by our grandparents. We lived across the street from eleven cousins. We are used to having a crowd.

Linda and Tory are now responsible for six children. Two of them, Tyler, eight, and Brandon, six, are their natural children. They have adopted three siblings from the foster care system: Carvel, eleven; Jasmine, ten; and Ashley, seven. The sixth child in their home is "K. K.," sixteen, who came to them via an informal, underground child welfare system based on relationships and compassion rather than laws and contracts. Tory's family has ties to K. K.'s parents. In high school, he baby-sat for the boy. K. K.'s mother "has issues," according to Linda. Rather than see him follow two of his sisters into foster care, she and Tory have served as his guardians for the last four years without any financial assistance from his real parents. "It's the same as if he were my own," Linda said.

The Hines's three adopted children were taken by court order from their birth mother, and then bounced around the foster care system for several years. Linda believes that the three siblings received little or no stimulation in foster care. They did not seem to understand even how to play with toys when they came to her. At first they destroyed those that she gave them. They also had seen little of the world. Today, the three children joke about the fact that when they first saw a cow, they did not know what it was. They called it a "Chicago bull." All three of the Hines's adopted kids have difficulty bonding with other people. The two oldest generally have little to do with the youngest, Ashley. They don't trust in relationships or in their own security. Each of them has taken food or candy and stashed it, as if fearful that there will come a time when they will not be fed.

Carvel, Jasmine, and Ashley were already living as foster children at Hope Meadows when Linda and Tory arrived. Initially they were placed with an older woman who, in spite of her best intentions, was finding it difficult to deal with them—particularly with Ashley and her fiery temperament. The woman had been getting support from other Hope families, including a couple who agreed to take in Ashley for a while to give her some relief. They found the girl to be a handful, too. At one point, Ashley chased the wife around the house while threatening her with a knife. On another occasion, Ashley threw a tantrum when the husband took her to Wal-Mart. People in the store called 911 after seeing the white man carrying a screaming little black girl out into the parking lot. Police surrounded the beleaguered father until he explained that he was a Hope Meadows parent looking after this raging child.

After her turbulent stay with that couple, Ashley rejoined her siblings and her original Hope foster mother for a brief time, but she proved to be too much for the woman to handle. Ashley could not stand school. She would run through the halls yelling and hitting teachers who tried to intercept her. Often, they sent her home by ten in the morning. She was bright and manipulative, refusing to give teachers her phone number or address. If they sent disciplinary notes home with her, she'd throw them in the cornfield.

The single mother could not keep up with Ashley and care for two other children. When Linda and Tory moved to Hope Meadows, they were asked to take over guardianship of her and her siblings. "They prepared me for Ashley. They said she wets the bed. She curses. She lies and she is a tyrant," Linda recalled. I said, "Okay, I'll take her, and her sister and brother, too."

Their history was shaky, to say the least. The mother used drugs while pregnant. Ashley was not tested when she was born because her mother left the hospital with her. All three kids were taken from the mother and put in foster care. I had to worry about Ashley's influence on my own son when she first came to us. She would fondle herself and try to coax the other children to do things. Once, she lifted her dress when she walked by K. K. I have to watch her with what I call my "superhawk vision." We put a Lion King alarm in her room that roared "Somebody has entered the pride lands" if she got out of bed at night, because she'd wander around the house. She will scratch herself, too, and then say she doesn't know how she got the scratches. She's been seeing an outside therapist because of the extent of her problems. The therapist said that's a sign that she doesn't like herself. That comes out, too, in the fact that for a long time, she couldn't take praise. Neither could Carvel or Jasmine. If you praised them, they immediately went downhill. With Ashley, her self-esteem was so low that if she got in trouble, she'd say, "You don't like me anymore." We had to work on getting her to understand that we could not like her actions, and still like her.

The private therapist has helped Ashley with "nurturing counseling" that lets her have some of the things she obviously missed in her earliest days. She will be allowed to have a baby bottle and to play with dolls in a nurturing manner, but if she mistreats the dolls they are taken away. That has happened several times already. But she has gotten better at understanding where the boundaries are for her behavior. She doesn't do well in school, though her therapists and tutors say she knows more

than she'll let you think. She comes home and does her numbers and colors but she won't do them at school.

Carvel has learning disabilities, and Jasmine is reluctant to form attachments with people, but their problems have been far more manageable than their youngest sibling's. In fact, Ashley's incendiary outbursts and deeply rooted problems nearly discouraged Linda, an optimist by nature, from going through with adoption proceedings for the children. The process had been started but Ashley "went haywire" and Linda became fearful that she might not be able to handle her over the long term. "I even talked about just adopting her siblings because she has no real attachment to them," Linda recalled. "If somebody told her she was cute and that they wanted to take her home, she'd say, 'Can I go?' "

"I told my pastor that I wasn't sure this was what God wanted me to do because I couldn't see that he'd want me to suffer with this kid," she noted. "I prayed and, finally, I decided that we should adopt them all." Even that step was made more difficult because of the tormented histories of Ashley and her siblings. It is not unusual for Hope children to have a considerable fear of police officers and their vehicles. Police forcibly removed many of them from their birth homes. Many lived in turbulent households in which domestic violence brought police officers to the door. But the staff workers at Hope Meadows have rarely seen children react so strongly to a courtroom as did Ashley and her siblings.

The Hines' described what was going to happen in court to prepare the children for the adoption proceedings. Ashley became terrified and said that she did not want to see a judge. "I don't want him hitting that thing," she said in apparent reference to the gavel. Her

brother and sister said they had the same fear. To calm the children, Linda and Tory asked that the judge refrain from using his gavel during the proceeding, and Linda wrote a note assuring them that they were loved and that after they went to court they could live together forever.

The adoption went smoothly. As often happens, the behaviors of Carvel and Jasmine improved significantly once they understood that they would never again be moved to another family. Ashley has continued to act out. She puts no stock in her own worth or her own judgment. If she wins a prize in school, she picks something not for herself, but for Linda. She will not pick out her own clothes, relying on Linda's tastes instead. She reacts in extremes to disapproval, out of fear that her adoptive mother will send her away or not love her anymore. She sees rejection everywhere.

She had impetigo, which is really contagious, on her lips about six months ago, and I told her I would give her a kiss on the cheek but she couldn't kiss me on the lips. I'm a diabetic and it's hard for me to get rid of things like that. So, for a whole week, it was horrid because she couldn't kiss me. She felt I didn't love her or care about her. She'd go to bed crying. She fought going to school. She'd pick at the sore on her lips and make it worse so that it spread. It took her a while to realize that she had to leave it alone. It was devastating for her and it put her back. We had to start building the relationship all over. Now she's back giving me kisses and she stays at my side constantly. We were discussing whether or not I needed a break from Ashley, but I said I'd never do it because whenever I leave her, she is ten times worse when I get back.

All in all, her behavior has begun to improve. At home, her tantrums are rare. She threw one the other day and I threw one right with her. When she saw me do it, she stopped. It was funny. I got down

and kicked and threw things around her room. I told her I didn't mind tearing up her things if she didn't.

Tory Hines works nights as a youth counselor at the Chanute Transition Center, a halfway house for juvenile offenders, located just a few blocks from Hope Meadows. Every day there, he witnesses what happens to abused and neglected children who never receive the support and guidance of committed guardians. "Some of the kids in the transition center have been in the system since they were very young, going from foster home to foster home. No one has taken the time to be a role model for them," he said.

As a result, Tory noted, they end up incarcerated and, worse, the cycle of abuse and neglect continues as they become parents themselves. "They tell me they are fathers and my answer to them is that if they are in prison, they aren't fathers. To be a father, you have to be involved in raising the child. Some of them wake up and realize what they need to do. Some don't. When I look at our kids at home, I often wonder where they would have ended up if we hadn't stepped in," he said. "From my work, I've learned that it's up to us to step up and make a change in their lives."

My dream was to have six children, but having a house big enough for them would have been an issue for us. We would not have been able to do it. Because of this place and the support it gives you, we can. And I love these kids. They are my everything. If you took them away, I would be nothing. I don't know what I would do. I spend all of my time playing baseball and double-dutch and having slumber parties. Our house is always full of kids.

I think I have some kind of extended patience, even though there are times when I think I'm at the end of my rope. Last winter, I walked out. I'd had it. I found out that Ashley had acted out sexually again and then lied to me about it. I lost it. I basically went off in a rage and I began to swear, which is very unlike me. My husband and son came running downstairs because they don't ever hear me talk like that. They told me to calm down and come upstairs, but I went out the door. It was freezing outside. There was snow on the ground. I didn't take a coat. And I didn't notice because I was so upset. I walked around for probably a half-hour. Then I cooled off and came back home. Sometimes with these kids, you need to get out of the house, and that was one of those times.

Can you believe that I'd like to adopt just one more? I am insane, really. I simply have no brains left, do I?

Chapter Seven

"I've Watched
This Man Come
Alive Again."

Before George and Effie King joined the first group of residents to move into Hope Meadows in 1994, doctors told George that he probably had only two years to live. Effie wasn't so sure their thirty-six-year marriage would last even that long. George was only sixty-five years old then, but he was letting himself get run-down and depressed. His hard-charging wife was rapidly losing patience with him. In his defense, George had a long series of health problems, including a collapsed lung and cardiovascular disease. But Effie's exasperation was due mostly to George's dark mood. "He just was not happy being alive," she said. "And I wasn't going to let him give up and die and leave me all alone."

George's flagging spirits were especially hard for her to take because at fifty-seven Effie was just picking up speed. Though she had never graduated from high school, she'd talked her way into Parkland Community College, where she was studying for an associate's degree. She was also working with disabled young adults in the community, teaching them how to live independently. Meanwhile, back home, her husband was becoming increasingly dependent. In exasperation, Effie had resorted to hiring a home health care nurse to do for George what he could not, or refused, to do for himself.

I was at the end of my rope with him. My life was very full. I'd get up in the morning and go to school and then go to work and come home at night, and George would just be sitting around all day. He needed so much of my attention, he was smothering me. He was underfoot and housebound. He was cooking up all the food in the refrigerator just to see how much he could eat in one day, trying to find fulfillment that way. I didn't know what to do with him and he didn't know what to do with me.

Effie is nearly six feet tall, with a confident, regal bearing and little tolerance for laggards especially within her immediate family. She grew up on "the prettiest ninety-two-acre farm in all of Mississippi," as the sixth of twelve children. She ruled from the middle, then and now. "I was always in the middle of the family, and of any arguments. I'm still the mediator today. That's my role in life. My mother was very delicate. My father was a wise man, who had a way of helping people find solutions to their own problems. I have my dad's genes. That wisdom passed on," she stated.

Effie met George—who was also Mississippi born, but raised in central Illinois—when he came to her family's door to sell Watkins spices and extracts. George was a handsome, broad-shouldered man who "smelled like vanilla," Effie fondly recalled. She went to work for him at the age of fifteen, and married him four years later in Champaign, Illinois.

They raised seven children: five girls and two boys of their own, and then two nephews as well. The Kings also served as foster parents for Catholic Social Services for more than twelve years. George worked at General Motors, and Effie did housekeeping, cooking, and child care for university couples and other professionals. Some might have considered it domestic work. Effie billed herself as "a family builder." Many of the families she worked with were dysfunctional, she explained, and they became reliant on her to help them resolve their issues. "In one way or another, I've always worked with troubled families in the community. Even pastors call me when they get in trouble."

When she learned of Hope Meadows, Effie was intrigued by its mission of nurturing troubled children, but she was also enticed by its affordable and safe housing. Seniors at Hope Meadows are candid about the fact that one of its greatest appeals is the relatively cheap and safe harbor it offers. Most are on fixed incomes, and there are few low-cost housing areas in central Illinois or elsewhere, with such protective and attentive neighbors.

We were living in a Champaign neighborhood that I was not pleased with. There was a lot of bad activity. I picked up the newspaper one day and the headline "Hope" jumped out at me. I had been praying for something different. I'm a firm believer that God has something better in mind for me. I had George call and get an interview, and we were the first seniors to pick out a home—we got the pick of the litter. Our life changed for the better from the day we moved in.

We feel so safe here and there is so much support and concern. The children leave May baskets on our doorstep and their parents call to check on us. It works both ways. A few weeks ago I ran into one of our Hope children who was in a semi-truck with a truck driver on the street. I did not know this truck driver, and he was letting one of our kids up in the truck. I didn't feel comfortable about it, and I asked the child if his parents knew where he was. He looked at me and said, "I go every-where!" I said, "That's not what I asked you. Do your parents know where you are?" And he said, "Nope." So I told him I was going to make sure they did know, and in the meantime, I wanted him out of that truck right now. I told him to get back across the street. Well, he wasn't sure I was gonna call over there, but I made sure I followed through. And he knew when the phone rang and my voice was on the phone. "Oh boy! That's Mrs. King."

The boy's parents were impressed that I'd taken time out of my evening walk to shoo this kid back across where he should have been. But to me, that's part of living here. Hope is a very challenging program. It's been everything that I ever dreamed of, and a great thing for George and me.

Effie works full-time as a counselor in a program for troubled youths in Rantoul, and she runs a crafts and secondhand store in its retail district. George helps out in the store, but mostly he is an enthusiastic volunteer at Hope Meadows. As Effie has noted, "George is kicking real high now." The elderly gentleman, who could hardly get out of bed five years ago, now works as a crossing guard at 7:30 each schoolday. When he leaves that post, he often goes to a playground where he supervises younger kids, and then he walks over to the Intergenerational Center at Hope Meadows where he visits with other senior residents. He takes a break in the early afternoon, and then reports for crossing-guard duty again when school lets out.

In his spare time, George, whose parents were both ministers, serves as the laypastor of the Twin City Apostolic Assembly Way of Holiness Church, which has a congregation of about fifty in Urbana. His son, George, Jr., a data analyst in Akron, Ohio, said that he's seen his father's mental and spiritual well-being improve dramatically since moving to Hope Meadows. While his parents have always been caring, spiritual people, he's seen them live their faith and deepen it. George, Sr., agrees.

Before I came here, I was in a state of withdrawal from the world. I was depressed. I felt there was nothing I could do. I wasn't accomplishing anything anymore. I was just surviving. But when I came here, I got involved immediately with the kids and the community and my life began to mean something. I had a goal—to help the kids—and that turned my life around. I didn't realize that I had anything to offer anymore until I came into the program here. I helped build the first float for our first parade here. I was part of the creation of our volunteer school patrol. I did the first enrichment hour. I've been part of everything that's been done here, and that's a great feeling.

This is a community that everyone is involved in. No one is isolated. And everyone is focused on the children. I have learned that children from broken homes often have never had the things our own children took for granted, and so we have to be patient with them. We have to understand that they never had parents who interacted with them and played with them, or showed them that they were loved. So we do that for them here. These children have been abused so much that they stand and look at you and in their minds they are wondering if you are for real, or just another adult putting on an act. But once they find out you are for real, you can make a difference. Like Effie says, these are not microwave kids. You can't push a button and expect everything to pop into place. You have to let them give you a sense of the direction they need. We have to show them that the seniors love them, and that where there is love there is understanding. We try to give them the best advice as far as the importance of school and an education.

I've learned from them, too. I see what these kids have endured and it makes me think that if they can go through that and find happiness, why can't we all accept hardship and endure misunderstanding and find happiness and peace, too?

Alexander was one of the children who did not find happiness at Hope Meadows in spite of the efforts of George King and several other Hope residents. Alexander came to the community as an adolescent, big for his age and with a seething, unpredictable rage. He'd entered the foster care system after alerting DCFS to violence in his own family. He was the whistle-blower, and as a result of his entirely justified actions, he and his siblings were taken out of the home. Still, Alexander felt tremendous guilt for that, even though it was the right thing to do. He packed a heavy burden of guilt and anger when he entered the child welfare system, and it did not serve him well. Because of his volatile temper, he was moved from one placement to the next for several years before coming to Hope Meadows.

Three different Hope Meadows families tried to work with Alexander, but his violent outbursts were more than they could handle, particularly because of the threat he posed to other children in the homes. He also caused problems in school, disrupting classes and running away. Authorities had threatened to expel him, but George King and another Hope senior, Eddie Foster, stepped up to try to help the boy stay in school. The two men took turns accompanying Alexander to school over several months. They sat with him during class and at lunch in an attempt to keep him from being disruptive. "He was a hard kid to get to," said King.

He had what I would call a split personality, because one minute he'd be one of the best young men you've ever been around, but then he could go into a terrible rage. I never had a serious problem with him, but he had given others problems. I worked with him one-on-one at the Intergenerational Center, too. He'd come and sit and talk with me at the center and I'd ask him questions about school and whether he enjoyed it. I tried to get him to realize that he was loved by the seniors and families at Hope. But I guess he never came to trust anyone. Not too many had showed him love in his life. He was one of those children who didn't want to be touched or bumped up against on the playground. I'd talk to him about that, but he'd had a hard time all of his life with people, I guess. His parents had never showed him the love they should have.

I know we did everything we could for that young man. You can't win them all. Some you are going to lose. It's sad that he had to leave here. He didn't know when he was well off. I'm told that he's in a children's home now and he asks about us more than any of the other people he'd been with over the years. So, he must have bonded with us. It wasn't a big bond, but we left a positive mark on his life.

You have to be willing to not expect too much too soon when you are working with troubled youths. You just work with every little bit that comes your way, everything they'll give you. But if you try to give them too much too soon, they can overreact. That's been my experience. You can't give them more than they can handle at any given time, just as you don't take a drugstore prescription all at once. You have to take one pill and let it work, and then wait until it's time for the next dose.

"Sometimes it's not medicine that heals a person. Sometimes it's not what the doctors say. Sometimes it's having your needs fulfilled," Essie said.

That's what happened with my husband. That man puts me to open shame now. He makes me tired just watching him. Brenda says she'd like to have a couple more men like him here at Hope. But I think they broke the mold.

Our life has been enriched in so many ways, but the most dramatic is the change in George. I call him my "Eveready Man" now. Like the battery, he never runs down. I've watched this man come alive again because of this place. It has been a godsend for him. I've realized that it really wasn't all this sickness that was keeping him down. It was loneliness. I'd leave in the morning to go to work and he'd be here all alone. Now, with the kids, he has a reason to get up. There is such peace and contentment and joy in our home now.

When we first moved in here, we still had the home care nurse coming every morning for him, but after we'd been here a few months, George told her that he'd no longer be needing her services. He said, "I've got things to do now," and that was the truth. I haven't come home to find him standing at the door waiting for me ever since. He had to have surgery a while back and after it was over, he jumped out of bed and said, "I can't lie around anymore, I've got too much to do at Hope."

He's too busy exploring his life to worry about other things now. And that has restored the balance for us. A couple is not you and me. It's "we." And now we are both enjoying discovering the program here.

Chapter Eight

"IT'S KIND OF LIKE

PLEASANTVILLE."

Seven baskets of children's clothes are stacked up in the living room of Michelle Roberts's Hope Meadows home. More kids' clothes lie around in neat piles. Outside the door to her kitchen, a tangle of tricycles, bicycles, Hot Wheels, and toys clog the driveway. This is hardly the life that Michelle's parents had planned for their bright, independent daughter as she was growing up in a California mountain resort community.

As a teen, Michelle successfully lobbied a reluctant local school board to gain admittance to another town's high school honors' program. After she won that campaign, it occurred to her parents that Michelle would probably make a fine lawyer. They envisioned her getting a law degree, having a career, and then starting a family. Instead, Michelle has made a career of providing for children without families. At only twenty-eight, this highly independent, resourceful, and caring young woman is the guardian of six girls rescued from the child welfare system. Two of her children were born to drug-addicted mothers. Two of them are teenagers who were neglected and abused by their own parents. Several of her girls have complex emotional and behavioral problems.

The odds are that none of them would have ever known a permanent home or a secure childhood if it were not for Michelle. Michelle first came to Hope Meadows in 1997, not as a resident, but as a part-time adoption counselor. Although single, and still in her early twenties, she was deeply involved in the child welfare system. At that point, she already was raising five foster children, including a cocaine-addicted infant she had accepted a few days after birth. The blond, blue-eyed baby named Olivia was going through a nightmarish withdrawal. To care for the addicted baby, Michelle left her full-time job with Lutheran Family Services and quit her studies for a master's degree in social work. To pay bills, she took the part-time job at Hope Meadows, but after only a few weeks, it was obvious that tiny, tormented Olivia needed all of her attention. Michelle was in a quandary. She still had the other children to care for, and living expenses to meet. Her solution was to stop working for Hope Meadows, and to become a resident instead.

Single mothers head a quarter of the households at Hope Meadows. Like Michelle Roberts, these women have found that the free housing, subsidies to stay-at-home parents, and support from foster grandparents and counselors make it possible for them to care for needy children. Even with subsidies and support, they often struggle. Yet, they remain committed to nurturing young people who have been cast off, abused, and neglected. By the time she was twenty-five years old, Michelle had served as a temporary foster mother to more than thirty youngsters. Until 1997, none of the children who came to her were eligible for adoption, but then within a fourteen-month period, she was allowed to adopt her five foster daughters. She has since taken in a sixth child—another cocaine-addicted baby—as a long-term foster placement, who she hopes to adopt one day. It would be no easy task for a single parent to raise her own six girls, but these children came into Michelle's care after they'd undergone considerable trauma at the hands of their natural parents, and sometimes their previous foster parents.

- After being in and out of foster care, Maggie, fifteen, petitioned a judge to take her from her large and troubled family.

- April, fifteen, and Keri, nine, are sisters who were left to fend for themselves in a chaotic household.

- Little is known about five-year-old Alyssa's past, but when she plays with dolls, this striking but stormy child often acts out dramas in which adults are the enemy and cannot be trusted.

- Olivia, three, Michelle's first cocaine baby, went through a tortured withdrawal in her first few months of life.

- Her youngest and most recent addition, Macy, is not yet a year old. She, too, was born with a cocaine addiction and while her withdrawal has been much milder than Olivia's, there are concerns that the long-term effects may be far more severe.

Michelle has taken on a great deal, but like many of the parents at Hope Meadows, she asks: "If I don't do it, who will?"

In the beginning, I wondered what I'd done, taking on all of these kids. It all just happened, one thing after the other. At first I thought, "Sure, I can take in one foster child," and then a few months go by and they are saying, "Why don't you take another one?" and it just kept happening that way.

I had been working for Lutheran Family Services and [I] was going to graduate school when they asked me to become a licensed foster parent. They needed someone who could take children on an emergency, short-term basis. I started doing that, but then they began asking me to take children for longer periods. Within my first year as a foster parent, I ended up with six kids. But it seemed natural. I always wanted to be a mom more than anything. That was always my big thing as I was growing up. I played with dolls until I was probably fifteen years old. I was the kid at family gatherings who wanted to play with the little kids and hold babies all the time.

My mother thought being a foster mother or adopting these kids was a terrible idea. But now, in the last couple years, she has said, "Obviously you know what works for you." She still thinks I'm nuts. Her big thing now is to say, "If you die, I'm going to kill you," because there is no way she wants to be responsible for six girls at this stage in her life.

Cindy Roberts, Michelle's mother, still lives in California where Michelle grew up in the resort community of Lake Arrowhead. Her daughter was a happy, confident child who became dissatisfied with the local high school in her junior year because it did not offer enough honors courses. She went before the board members of a San Bernardino high school and convinced them to let her enroll in the honors program there. "She'd been turned down initially so she had to go back to the principal and then to the board members to plead her case. I didn't really want her driving down the mountain to school every day, but she convinced the board that she wanted to learn. They let her in and the school loved her," said Cindy Roberts.

"After that, I was sure she'd become an attorney. My plan for her was career, marriage, and then family," the mother said. "Instead she has made a career out of family. She is a very happy person, so I think she is doing the right thing for her. I've learned you can't direct your children's lives. We are not the engineers of this train. I'm just glad she is her own person, independent and creative, and lucky in a lot of ways."

Single motherhood was never really Michelle's plan either. She was dating someone seriously when she had just three foster girls, but her boyfriend was opposed to her taking any more foster children. When she could not turn down the deeply troubled Olivia, their relationship ended.

I haven't dated since, but I've gotten more kids. It takes so much energy to do this. I don't feel like I have any left for a relationship. I feel like I'm overcommitted to this and to put energy and time into something else would be overwhelming. I think about getting married way in the future, like a second life when the girls are grown. I think it would be really hard now to find anybody willing to take on six kids. And if I did, I'd have to question his motives. I did it, but I didn't take them all at one time. I also think it would be hard for me to adjust to having a husband in the house. I'm used to being in charge and doing things my own way. It would be tough to share some of that power. It would be hard for the girls, too. I made my choices and I'm happy with them. Of course, there are trade-offs and things I gave up, but I don't spend my time thinking about that.

Michelle's life is wrapped up in her children now. The first of them to come under her care were April and Keri, who are siblings. Along with an older sister they came to Michelle as temporary foster placements in 1993, but left after a month when the court ordered them returned to their mother's care over the protests of the Department of Children and Family Services. A family-court judge had ruled that the DCFS did not prove that the girls were being neglected.

It might have ended there, if a determined college intern with the DCFS had not made it her mission to document the turmoil that existed in the family. The intern spent more than six months putting the case together. With the documentation, the DCFS was able to remove the girls and return them to Michelle's care. Nearly a year later, their mother agreed to terminate her parental rights.

By the time April and Keri were available for adoption they already seemed like my kids. There was never a question about whether or not to adopt them. They were the first kids I'd cared for who became eligible. April was nine, then. Keri was three. April had a big problem with her temper. She would lash out. There was evidence of neglect. They were left on their own a lot. April and her older sister were often kicked out of the house. They wouldn't come back until night.

April wasn't attached to anybody. She kept in her own little world. It was like she was just visiting us. The first couple of years that I had her, people would say the whole family clicks except for April who doesn't seem part of the family. She was only nine, but back then she thought she should be able to date. She wanted to wear makeup. The environment she'd come from had been inappropriate. The kids were treated like they were adults.

Soon after I got her, April went in for a psychological evaluation and the psychologist said, "You are going to have problems with her. She thinks she is so much older than she is." The psychologist didn't have much hope, but after her mother's rights were terminated, there was an amazing transformation in April. I had her older sister at the time, too, but when their natural mother terminated her rights as a parent, the older sister, who had initially pushed to be adopted, became highly emotional and opposed to adoption. She felt like she was betraying her mom. She ended up going elsewhere as a foster child until she turned eighteen. April didn't want to be adopted at first either, but when her mother gave up rights, it was as if the walls had come down. She started bonding with me and our family here, and suddenly it felt like she belonged. She did a total turnaround. She calmed down a lot. She still has a temper, but she's learned how to control it better. She began acting more appropriate for her age, and she really got to, finally, be a kid.

If you had told me six years ago she would be doing this well I would not have believed it. She is still a normal teenager who drives me crazy most of the time, but she has just really turned her life around.

April, fifteen, is Michelle's pretty, "All-American girl." She has a self-deprecating sense of humor and an engaging frankness, though she tends to be shy. She was diagnosed as learning disabled, but with tutoring and special help, she has done well in school. Recently she made the school's dance squad, which performs at athletic events. With typical candor, April describes her life before coming to Hope Meadows as "very ghetto."

We lived in this nice house but it flooded. The Red Cross helped us but money was always scarce. We always shopped for clothes at the Salvation Army. It seemed like my stepdad and mom fought all the time. I think I must have gone to every women's shelter in the state with my mom and my sisters. My mom would sometimes threaten that she was going to kill herself. Then one day, we went to a women's shelter and they figured out there was something wrong with my mom. So me and my sister Keri and our older sister, Joy, had to go to a foster home. It was late at night; we came to Michelle's house and the DCFS caseworker asked her if she'd take us. Michelle said yes, but we only stayed for a month before we went back home. I remember I was in my fourth-grade class and the principal made an announcement on the intercom telling me to see him. I went to his office and he said, "Your mom needs help so she is going to be at the hospital, and you'll go back to your foster parent." I was so sad at that time. I had to leave all my friends and stuff.

At first, I didn't go to Michelle's because Michelle had too many kids. I went to another place and I was depressed. Michelle had a lot of kids but her foster home was really good. The other place was weird. They let their kids smoke. After two months or something, Michelle lost some kids and I got to go back to her and live with my sisters. I stayed with her in fourth and fifth grade and then in sixth grade my mom gave up her rights. My older sister was a teenager at the time and she had to make the decision whether she wanted to be adopted or not. She decided she didn't want to be adopted. She lives on her own now and she regrets saying no about getting adopted. She thought there was something better, but there wasn't. She went from foster home to foster home and now she lives in her own apartment, and she has a car and a job. I don't know if she will go to college or not. She is always sad and depressed because she had a chance to be with us.

I think life is better now. I'm with one of my sisters and I see my mom once or twice a month and I talk to my older sister all the time. Life is calmer. When I was young, I didn't have a lot of things like my little sisters here do now. They have everything. They get clothes every day. I'm not ghetto anymore.

It is difficult to believe that April's little sister, Keri, was once so lethargic and unresponsive that Michelle feared she was autistic. Today, this little live wire stops chattering only long enough to think of a new question to ask of her mother or to offer a reading from the books she brings home and pores over. This once severely distressed child has blossomed into an irrepressible dynamo, hungry for knowledge and excited about the world that has opened to her.

Keri was just a toddler when I got her. She did not interact with anybody. She was almost like a little zombie. She'd just stare into space for hours and hours. We found that she was dehydrated so I took her to the doctor. They wanted to hook her up to an IV but they couldn't find a vein. They kept poking her over and over, moving from her arms to her feet. She let them poke her but she didn't cry. Then she sat there for two hours with an IV in her foot. She didn't move or say anything. How many kids would respond like that?

When she and her sisters had to go back to their parents because of the court order, my own mom said she was glad they were leaving because she thought there was something seriously wrong with Keri. Nine months later, they came back to me and Keri was the same. She was incredibly shy. She hid behind my legs and held tight to my clothes when other people were around.

I think she was extremely neglected. Right before Keri was born, her mother met a new guy and married him and then had Keri. Nine months later, she had another baby, and a year after that, another one. The stepfather was interested in his own kids and the others, including Keri and April, were often left on their own.

When they first came, I asked April what time Keri took a nap. She said, "Whenever she falls asleep in front of the TV." I think she had no stimulation at all. Once she got it, she made an amazing turnaround. It's an interesting look at the nature or nurture question. Most of her family had low IQs but Keri tested at 121. Genetically, that doesn't seem possible. Keri is a voracious reader. I can't keep the kid in books. From the first grade, she was reading the same books her older sister read, and now in the third grade she's reading Harry Potter books passed to her by Maggie. Last year in the second grade, she read the entire *Little House on the Prairie* series, and her reading level was fifth grade, third month.

Keri is one of the most well-adjusted kids in the family. I feel I got her in time. She was young enough that I could really make a difference. This is her family now, and she doesn't have the issues that the older kids might have after leading pretty tumultuous lives. Now, when you meet her, she never stops talking. I think she is making up for lost time.

> Michelle Roberts's spot in heaven may be reserved, not only because she has taken in six girls, but because two of them are now fifteen years old and armed with driver's permits. Teens Maggie and April are from different families but share backgrounds of neglect. They have responded to the security of a permanent home by becoming typical teenagers—a relative luxury for young people from shattered families. "When I took Maggie, my mom was livid. She thought it was horrible, having two girls the same age. She felt I'd set up a really bad situation," Michelle said. She describes April and Maggie as "typical sisters" but notes that in some ways they are like twins. They share friends and are involved in many of the same school activities, but they are very different people who do get on each other's nerves occasionally. "They wouldn't be friends if they just knew each other in school, but they have been thrown together and they really enjoy each other," Michelle said. "I think they are really close and care about each other. They get along ninety percent of the time."

The girls don't seem to compete against each other so much as hold each other up. Maggie just shines, but she makes sure that April gets her share of the limelight, too. Maggie really tries to help April out. Maggie is involved in everything and gets all kinds of awards and is on the honor roll, and Maggie is aware how that must seem to April, so she is good at pointing out the things April is good at, too. They really do both shine in their own ways. April is really pretty and has every guy at that school following her around like puppies.

> April and Maggie knew each other from school before they lived together as adopted sisters. As Michelle noted, they might never have become friends if they hadn't been thrown together in the same pieced-together family. Yet, their shared backgrounds give them an unusual bond, which seems to give both of them strength. "We are like, best friends," notes April. "We share clothes and borrow things. Maggie's the brains in the family. I'm smart, just not the brains."
>
> Maggie's story is compelling, but not unusual at Hope Meadows. At Hope, children aren't struggling just to survive. They are able to live and flourish like Maggie, who is "the comeback kid," according to Michelle.

I got Maggie when she was twelve. She is like the poster child for resiliency. She spent a long time in foster care because she was caught in a war between her mom and dad. She went back and forth. She was put in foster care at ten and was there for two years, and then sent home.

Shortly after I got her, the DCFS filed for termination of her parents' rights. The case became very political. It went on for a year and a half. The parents seemed to have the upperhand on DCFS and they won a termination hearing. There were eight kids in the family. Maggie was the second oldest. The judge said they had to go home to their parents. But Maggie fought to stay here. She did not want to go home. She wrote letters to the judge and her parents. We got her a psychiatric evaluation and the psychiatrist said she should not go home. Everybody at Hope Meadows fought for Maggie, and in the end she won. In court, the judge said that after all she had been through in her life, she deserved the opportunity to be in a place where there was hope.

Finally, last January, I got guardianship of her and got her out of the foster care system. She'd spent five years in foster care. Like I said, if you looked up resiliency in the dictionary, there would be a picture of her. She is amazingly well-adjusted. I think she had incredible potential and she has been able to realize that potential here, but it's been almost all of her own doing. She was in the school play. She's on the speech team. She's in the National Honor Society and in the band, chorus, and madrigal singers. That's amazing. I just gave her the opportunity. She did the rest.

Maggie is a lanky, winsome brunette with a quick mind and sardonic wit. She still refers to herself occasionally as "a screwed-up foster child" though she appears to have left that part of her life well behind. Before entering the child welfare system, Maggie lived with her father and stepmother. "I wasn't allowed to go many places and I never joined any school activities even though I would have ripped my left arm off to just have some friends—maybe even my right arm, too." Maggie said her stepmother expected her to take care of her three younger siblings and the household. "I lost most of my childhood growing up too fast," she said.

When I first went into foster care, I didn't understand that my parents had done anything wrong. I thought, "They always do this, what's wrong with it?" I liked the way things were when I was younger. I was more free than anybody I knew. My parents were charged with neglect because they didn't watch us. I could go anywhere I wanted for the longest times. I walked all around town. It was fun then. I don't know if I would want to do it now. I don't know if I would let my kids do that. I don't think I would.

I didn't want to be in foster care. I had been in one foster home where all I did was clean. I was so relieved to get out of there. But my parents messed up again and I was sent back into foster care. I went to Michelle's house and realized that April lived there, and it was "Oh God, it's *her* house. I can't do it." But we were pretty nice to each other. We didn't claw out each other's eyes.

When my parents' rights were going to be terminated, I thought, "Oh, my God, what am I supposed to do?" then I realized, I liked being here with Michelle. When I was thirteen and still in foster care, I wanted to petition not to go home, but my dad wanted me to go home so I had to fight by going to court. My stepmom can't stand me and she makes it plainly known. There were a lot of things that happened in the past— bad stuff. I don't know if I could go back and just live with it. So I'm here. I couldn't get adopted so I'm under guardianship. Michelle really cares about me. My stepmom couldn't care less. My dad just wanted me because I was his kid. Go figure.

If I had to compare Hope to anything, I'd say it's kind of like *Pleasantville*, the movie. All the neighbors talk to each other. They have big barbecues together. It's safe here. When I'm here I think of myself as a Hope kid, but when I'm with a friend or at school, I think of myself as a normal kid. And that's a good thing, it's what I always wanted. Honestly, I never let myself think that I was abnormal, but I would watch *Full House* and *The Brady Bunch* reruns and thought, Why should I be any different from D.J. or Jan? I saw their on-screen lives and said that's what I'm gonna do. I hate when somebody tells me that I can't do something. It's kind of a pet peeve. I do what no one is expecting. If everyone expects me to fail at something, I'll go out of my way to do better than I can. Since I'm just some screwed-up foster child, and everyone told me that I couldn't ever do anything right, I've decided to prove them wrong, which is one of my fave things to do, just ask Michelle.

It took me a long time to find out that the world wasn't against me, I was against the world. That's one of the hardest concepts I've ever had to learn. Once I learned it, it made life so much easier. And I smile more now.

There are many wounded children at Hope Meadows. Quite often, beautiful young faces mask dark histories and troubled hearts. Five-year-old Alyssa Roberts is such a child. She has light, coffee-colored skin, long black curly hair, thick black eyebrows, and eyelashes over wide black eyes that can shine with youthful exuberance, or flash with fierce moodiness. "Alyssa is my neediest child," said Michelle.

I got her when she was seventeen months old. I have no idea what happened to her in those first months of her life, but it was bad. She had thirteen brothers and sisters, and all eight of the juveniles had already been put in foster care before she was born. DCFS removed the other kids while the mom was pregnant with her. I think it was a major mistake. They had the idea that if they took the others, the baby might have a chance. But the parents were drug addicts and the mom was severely depressed. There was a lot of domestic violence, a lot of chaos and physical abuse, and they left this baby there. They only took her out of the home when the mother called and said, "Come and get her, I don't want her anymore."

Alyssa has an inability to form attachments with people. She views parents as negative people who don't take care of you. She had a psychological evaluation when she was four. They were playing this therapy game with doll characters of different ages and Alyssa could pick characters and tell a story. Typically, kids choose a character of their own age. Alyssa always chose a baby. Her stories were always about babies being hurt or chased by monsters, and no adults being there to save the babies. That is how she views the world. It shows that a child's earliest months are so significant. It's so hard to undo what was done in those first seventeen months. I've had her nearly three years and I'd say she has made a little progress.

Alyssa has built a protective shell. She is very standoffish. My daughter Olivia is a typical preschooler who always wants to sit in my lap. Alyssa rarely does that. She used to sit in the backseat of our van with Keri, but they fought constantly so I changed the seats around. I put Olivia back there with her. She fought with Olivia the whole time. I was getting so frustrated. I said I was going to have to put her on the roof because she wasn't getting along with anybody. She is just difficult, that's the best word to describe her right now.

They say that eventually time and nurturing and care will change her view, but the research isn't real positive about children with attachment issues. It is a pretty major thing and they don't really know a lot about it. She has been too young for therapy, but now she will start seeing the Hope counselor. My mom was opposed to my adopting Alyssa. I had a brother who was a difficult person from the time he was a baby. My mom said he was her cross to bear, but he was her child. She couldn't understand why I would choose to adopt Alyssa when I knew she was so difficult. I have a couple of answers to that question. The first is, "If not me, then who?" I think I am a pretty skilled parent with my background, more skilled than most, anyway. I think that if anybody can help her I can. And, I have always felt that once a child is in my home, she is my kid. I have hope for her. She has a lot of potential and I hope she can be a successful person someday.

Olivia, the child whose severe drug withdrawal problems brought Michelle to Hope Meadows is now a lively charmer with blond curls tumbling to her shoulders. The three-year-old is a favorite of the seniors at the Hope Meadows Intergenerational Center because of her sweet temperament. As an infant, she was a bundle of exposed nerves. The slightest noise or movement threw her into meltdown. Such a child can be impossible to place in foster care, and especially in adoption. The challenges are just too great for most foster or adoptive parents. Fortunately for Olivia, Michelle Roberts is an exceptional caregiver, and Hope Meadows provides her with the opportunity to do what she does best.

As Michelle described her early struggles with Olivia, the now healthy and thriving little girl dressed in red overalls played intently with brightly colored Play-Doh molds, blissfully unaware of what her life might have been like if not for this woman and the community dedicated to helping her. "Olivia is simply an amazing kid, who had a terrible start in life," said Michelle.

Olivia is the reason we are here at Hope Meadows. I also joke that she's the reason I don't have a master's degree. She was an extremely difficult baby. She had a variety of sensory problems as a result of her drug exposure. You couldn't whisper around her, she was so sensitive to sound. The other kids would walk around going "Shhhh . . . ," not wanting to upset her because she would get hysterical. She was one of several children. The others also had been adopted. When Olivia was born the hospital didn't test her for cocaine exposure. They were going to release her with the mother until the mother's brother asked the nurses if they were aware of her drug history. Olivia was tested then and sure enough, she was cocaine exposed, so they took her and the mother surrendered her parental rights. The man alleged to be her father denied she was his child and surrendered rights, too. I was able to adopt her at eleven months.

Her first year was very rough because of all the sensory stuff. She got really behind developmentally because she had to struggle so much just to deal with the withdrawal. But she caught up almost completely by the time she was two. Her birth mom was actually more of an alcoholic than a drug addict and that was the biggest concern.

Cocaine does a lot of damage at the beginning, but alcohol has the long-term effects, so Olivia has been monitored by a geneticist. They don't understand fetal alcohol syndrome at all. Some kids will be severely damaged while others will turn out okay. Cognitively, Olivia is right there with her age group and very outgoing. Her only problem now is some mild speech delays. She has turned out amazingly well.

Michelle's most recently arrived foster child, Macy, was also born to an addicted mother. While Olivia was an inconsolable screamer, and sensitive to everything around her when she first came to Michelle, this child has shown few obvious problems. But Macy's lack of progress physically and mentally has become more and more disturbing, particularly since the levels of cocaine in her system at birth were reportedly the highest the public health department had ever seen.

There hasn't been a lot of research on cocaine babies, but she does not seem to be typical. She sleeps a lot and is not very highstrung or oversensitive to stimulation. I'm wondering if the cocaine has had a different effect on her. Ritalin is a stimulant that they use to calm people down, and maybe the cocaine has had that effect on her. I don't know what accounts for the difference, but she has not been a great deal of trouble. She is developmentally delayed and has been in a lot of occupational, developmental, and speech therapy. We've done a lot of testing trying to figure out what is going on with her. The cocaine is out of her system but she still has side effects. She had been lethargic and zombielike, as if she'd been in a deep sleep, but now that is fading and she is interacting more, but she is still different. They don't know what is wrong. She doesn't respond like most babies. She isn't smiling or cooing yet.

> Michelle had planned to adopt her youngest girl if the child became eligible for adoption, in spite of the potential for long-term problems but as the summer of 2000 began, it became increasingly obvious that Macy's development was not simply delayed. "She hasn't been developing at all," said the concerned guardian.

At eight months old, she was still at the one-month level of development. Typically, cocaine babies are delayed, but it is a consistent delay. They are always a few months behind, but they do progress consistently. With Macy, the gap just keeps getting bigger and bigger. I kept thinking that there was something more going on with her than her exposure to cocaine. She was just shut down, like someone who was doped up. She was never very responsive, and everybody who interacted with her said there seemed to be something seriously wrong. One woman here, who had worked with mentally handicapped adults in a previous job, said she could see that in her.

I'd been taking her to a lot of specialists, and the most recent was a neurologist who thought she may have been affected by something else in her mother's system before she was born. I reported that to Macy's caseworkers and as a result, her birth mother was interviewed. They found out she was taking antiseizure drugs while she was pregnant. I researched that on the Internet and found that those drugs can cause delayed development and mental handicaps. The average IQ for people with this syndrome is only 70. I started talking to therapists and they told me what was involved in caring for a child with this problem; they told me Macy would need extensive therapy for a long time.

The neurologist said Macy could be five years old and unable to walk. She would be severely disabled. The amount of time and energy she would need would take so much time away from my other kids, and it would change our lives so much, I had to make a decision. It was heartbreaking, the hardest decision I've ever made, but I finally decided that it would be unfair to the other kids because I would not be able to give them what they need. So, I decided not to adopt her and to find a new home for her. Personally, I would be willing to sacrifice a lot of myself and a lot of other things for Macy, but it wasn't fair that the other kids—the ones I have already adopted—should have to give up things.

I was worried about telling the other girls that Macy was not staying with us. I didn't want them to think they might have to leave, too, especially Alyssa, who is insecure as it is, but the counselor talked with her and said it didn't seem like she was disturbed. She understood that she has been adopted, but Macy hadn't been adopted. On some level the kids here are used to seeing children coming and going because most of them have been in foster homes where this was common. It's a sad fact of life for them.

Within just a few weeks, Michelle and the staff of Hope Meadows placed Macy in a foster home in Rantoul operated by a registered nurse, who specializes in caring for foster children with severe mental handicaps. As long as she remains in the child welfare system, Macy's medical expenses, which promise to be extensive, will be paid for by the state. If Michelle had adopted her, the medical costs would have been a considerable burden. Even with subsidies from Hope Meadows, Michelle has a monthly income of only about $2,000. Like many of the parents at Hope Meadows, Michelle is very creative in managing her budget, and in finding ways to support her adopted children. While she is a bit wary of sharing her secrets with anyone outside her circle of friends at Hope Meadows, it is well known there that she is a wizard at milking money from the World

Wide Web. Her skill at finding "freebies" and discounted goods on the Web is the subject of awe among her friends. The Roberts women had a major league windfall, for example, when Mark Mc-Gwire hit his record-breaking sixty-second homerun during a Cardinals-Cubs game on September 9th, 1998. She and her girls were in the stands. Their ticket stubs were suddenly part of history, and worth a considerable amount to collectors. Michelle managed to swap them for a cruise vacation for herself and her girls.

I am a bargain hunter. When people ask how I can afford to take the girls on cruises and vacation trips, I tell them that it's just a matter of hunting the bargains down on the Internet. When we go on our cruises, we go in the middle of November, which is the cheapest time of the year to go. I'm also on all sorts of e-mail lists for bargain hunters. When a company makes a special discount offer, or puts out a coupon on the Internet, everyone on the e-mail list is notified. Then you have to hunt it down. I pretty much had a cost-free Christmas thanks to the Internet. There were a lot of really good deals and when people found them, they notified the e-mail lists. I'd get on late at night when the girls were asleep and hunt them down. It was like an addiction there for a while: "Wow, here's another great deal!" There were a lot of retailers trying to draw people to their Websites to promote Internet shopping, so they'd offer $20 off on items starting at $20. If you bought a $20 item, then it was free. They were basically giving things away to get you to shop on their Website. It was great! Barnes & Noble and Amazon.com offered $10 gift certificates for registering on their sites, so I registered myself and all of the girls under their individual Web addresses—that was $70 right there.

The Internet also has sites that identify typos in online catalogs, and if you get there quickly enough, you can get the item for the lower price. One site had Nintendo 64 at $9.99 instead of $99.99, but I missed out on that one. I also missed it when the Gap had bras marked for 14 cents instead of $14. But I did get in on a deal when Toys "R" Us mismarked something by $40 but instead of letting you buy it at the lower price, they sent you a $40 gift certificate instead. I used that to order something else, and when it didn't come on time for Christmas, they gave me a $100 gift certificate. So that worked out really well.

> Living at Hope Meadows has allowed Michelle to help far more needy young people than she could otherwise have done on her own. For all of its blessings, Hope Meadows is still a work in progress, she notes. She does not want it to be idealized or glorified. She and other parents—and the seniors, too—feel they should have more input into decisions made that affect their lives and the lives of their families, something Brenda Eheart and others at Hope have vowed to work on.
>
> "I liken the process to being a parent. In the beginning you have to have a lot of control because you are training children, but then they will eventually reach a point when they can make decisions on their own, and you have to let them do it," Michelle said.

We are all so into promoting how wonderful Hope is, but there is good and bad about it. There are really great things it provides, such as allowing me to be a stay-at-home parent, which I feel is essential for Olivia and my other kids, too. It has benefited everybody for me to be at home and for that, I am so grateful. I think we should transform the whole foster care system into something in which people are paid for the time and effort they put into it. I think if you allow us to put our whole lives into helping these kids, you will end up with a much better system.

My kids are doing amazingly well. I think it would be interesting to compare them to kids with similar backgrounds who have remained in the foster care system. I think Hope has made a significant difference in their lives. I think having the seniors is wonderful. For them to be able to live in a place where they know everybody in the neighborhood and where they feel safe and needed is a great thing.

In parent-training classes recently we were talking about what age children should be before it is safe to leave them alone in the house, and how it is so much safer here than in most communities because I can depend on my neighbors. If I left Keri home, she could run to the Davises or the Calhouns and there would be somebody to help her. You don't have that in most communities. She was selling candy bars yesterday and it was so nice to be able to allow her to go from door-to-door. It's like a safe zone. They have so much more freedom than if they lived in another community, and it gives them a sense of security and belonging. They feel they are part of something here. I don't think they identify themselves as Hope kids, but they don't think of themselves as adopted kids either. Like most kids, they just want to be normal. Here that is possible because in our neighborhood every family has kids who are adopted. Everybody has kids who are different races, too. While they know that the rest of the world isn't like this place, they live where people are like them, with lives like theirs, and that is very nice for them. And life is never dull at Hope Meadows.

Chapter Nine

"I HAVE COME HOME,
I GUESS."

The old farmhouse on fifty acres of thick backwoods was a sheltering place in the rugged, tumbling terrain of Rutherford County, Tennessee, nearly sixty years ago. It was tucked into a sharp half-mile curve in the track of the Louisville and Nashville Railroad, which nearly every day carried raw black rock from the mines of Appalachia to the ever-hungry power plants of the Northeast. But not all of the ore completed the journey. Each coal car that hit the curve near the front stoop of the old Biederman place was jostled and frisked of some of its inky fragments, spilling them along the tracks for easy pickup by young Billy Biederman and his sister Deanna Delores. They felt it was God's way of giving back some of the native rock to warm their homes and those of their neighbors. The ready supply of coal inspired a stove or fireplace in nearly every room of their grandfather's house, which had eighteen rooms to begin with and kept growing as the family did.

The owner of the house was Emile John Biederman, who was born in Wiesbaden but became a proud German-Jewish-American. "He always claimed all three," his grandson Bill Biederman recalled.

Emile was a brewmaster for Nashville's William Gerst Brewery. His wife, Estella Lester, was a first-generation Irish-American out of County Cork. They'd come across the ocean to the United States as children at the same time, and on the same boat. They met years later in Rutherford County and there they married and raised three sons and three daughters. Most of the Biederman offspring moved out of the house during courting, and then moved back in with their spouses to build nest eggs for their own homes. Each time one of them returned, Emile tacked another room onto the house. Billy and Deanna Delores were the only grandchildren to become permanent residents. They were left behind when their mother and father departed packing separate suitcases.

Billy was three, his sister two, when their parents divorced. Their father went off to work in the steel mills of Gary, Indiana. Their mother headed for Nashville to work as a seamstress. Their parents were apart for twenty years before reuniting, remarrying, and stay-ing together for twenty more. In the marital interim, Billy and Deanna Delores were raised by their grandparents, uncles, and aunts in the big house along the tracks coated in coal soot. It was a boisterous, brawny place scented with four-inch blocks of Limburger cheese ("I still love the damn stuff. It's like eating birthday cake to me!" Bill says today.), hefty loaves of German rye, and sweaty buckets of Gerst beer brought home by Grandpa and his boys (several of whom also worked in the brewery). Every Friday night was celebrated as Men's Night.

Emile Biederman was a stocky, powerfully built leader of the household, who happily served as father to his grandson, protecting him and preparing him for life beyond the thick woods. Billy was a small, wiry boy who had to grow into his first rifle, though once he did, no squirrel, rabbit, or raccoon within thirty miles was allowed peace of mind. Bill Biederman grew up with a weapon on his shoulder, and uneasiness in his heart, he said.

I knew my grandmother and grandfather and all my aunts and uncles cared about us, but we didn't have a mother and father like the other guys and gals around the hills, and for a long time, I couldn't figure out why my parents didn't care for us. It probably wasn't that my parents didn't love us, but that's what it seemed like at the time. At least my grandparents were there to step in. My grandfather was really supportive of my sister and me. My grandmother was, too. Nobody could hurt us or correct us. In later years, one of my older aunts took over the job and finished raising us until we were out of the house. I was raised by family then, and now I'm the grandfather to this bunch here at Hope Meadows . . .

Bill Biederman's left forearm carries a faded reminder that his journey from his grandfather's house in rural Tennessee to Hope Meadows was by no means a direct or smooth route. The "Wild Bill" tattoo is a memento of his tours of duty as a sharpshooter for the U.S. Army's 101st Airborne. He went into the service at the age of sixteen after a Rutherford County judge signed his enlistment papers. The judge figured it was better than signing the teenager's death certificate. Billy Biederman, it seemed, had advanced from hunting squirrels and raccoons to poaching moonshine.

I'd married for the first time at sixteen, and there wasn't much to do in the hills so myself and eight other guys were stealing 'shine from the moonshiners and selling it. We had a great thing going. We'd steal it in gallon jugs and put it in half-pint jars and sell it for two and a half dollars a jar. We were teenagers then but we always had money. For a long time, the moonshiners thought it was Kentuckians coming over. They had no idea it was us. We got a lot of guns and rifles, too, because they'd put theirs with the 'shine and wrap the whole mess up in blankets and bury it. Hell, they'd even try to hide it in big hollowed-out trees. They'd tie a string around the top of each bottle and drop them down inside the trees so only the strings were hanging out. We'd go through the woods banging on tree trunks with big sticks and listening for hollow sounds. Sometimes they'd hide their stash in haylofts or under stairs or in the floors of their barns, in the trunks of old cars, too. We'd find their liquor everywhere. The moonshine was pure alcohol, 160, 170 proof pure grain. We tried to drink it some but it burned all the way down into your stomach and we didn't like that. We did like the money we made—until we got caught a couple times. The sheriff and the judge were friends of the moonshiners, and the second time we got caught, the judge said he was tired of the whole mess. He said he was either going to send us to jail for a long time, or he'd sign our enlistment papers and send us to Fort Campbell. And that's what he did. Eight of us went in and only three of us came home. We joined a group of about thirty other Tennessee misfits in a special detention barracks and had to go through Force Recon survival training.

Biederman was wounded several times during his military career, which he does not like to discuss, but he survived sixteen years of service and at least two "police actions" overseas. By the time he left the Army, he had a son, four daughters, and a marriage on the rocks. His teenage bride had found a life of her own as a Nashville songwriter, and their marriage disintegrated. He left the service with a commission as U.S. marshal in Nashville, but he'd been in that job only a short time when he came to Rantoul in 1969 to visit friends at Chanute Field. There, in the Officers' Club, he met his future second wife, Fran, and he decided to stay.

Weary of government service, he took a job as a diesel mechanic trainee at RW Regal Motortrucks. He worked there for nearly seventeen years, until he suffered the first of several heart attacks at the age of forty-nine. The heart problems left him unable to do the heavy lifting required in diesel repair so he went on disability, and, after a second heart attack in 1993, slipped into despondency. "Bill was down and out. He was taking a lot of medicine and that didn't help," said his wife, Fran, who has worked for twenty-seven years as a secretary for the National Council of Teachers of English in Urbana. "Bill is not a guy who can get used to sitting around. Before we moved to Hope, he didn't have enough to keep him busy and he did a lot of worrying about his health. Since we've moved to Hope, he has changed dramatically for the better."

Just as the Rutherford County judge forced him to enlist for military service to save his skin, Biederman's wife signed him up to become a Hope Meadows foster grandparent to combat his malaise. Now, at sixty-three, he acknowledges that it was a great move. Moving into Hope Meadows has been very much like going home again, he said. Within this community, Biederman has found a supportive, familial environment similar to the one he had as a boy in his grandparents' house. Only this time, he has taken on the role of mentor and guide for the needy children around him.

I'd mostly been sitting home feeling sorry for myself before we moved to Hope. I couldn't work for fear of having another heart attack. Fran wanted to get me up and going again. Living here has done that. It's giving me something to do. I'm helping these kids. There is a general loving and caring for each other here. The seniors take care of the children and vice versa. If a senior gets sick and has to go to the hospital, the foster parents are right there to help them out. It is like a caring village of the 1800s, and like the place I grew up. Everybody cares about each other and it's not made up. You can see it in the picnics and outings we have. I told Brenda Eheart once that she may know how many people she's thrown together, but she'll never know how many hearts she's put together. A lot of these children have never known a father or grandmother or grandfather and they eat up the attention they get from people who will keep them on the right path.

Sometimes it can be a challenge because when kids first come here out of the foster care system, they have a lot of problems. It was kind of a shock to me at first. Fran and I raised two of my daughters and three of her boys, and I can't believe what some of the parents of these kids have done to them. There are kids here who were beaten just because they were born. It shocks me that people would abuse a child sexually. These kids have had things done to them that the average person wouldn't even think of doing to a child. That's why so many of them, when they first come, won't let you touch them. If you do, they'll jerk away. I've seen them go backwards over in a chair rather than let someone pick them up.

We've had six or eight kids come in who've been really wild. After so many beatings and confrontations with adults, they go on the defensive. They have to look out for themselves. It's a sad thing. There was one eight- or nine-year-old girl who could talk to you like a prostitute. There was a little boy who cursed like he was in the Army. He taught me some stuff I'd never heard before, and he was only about six years old. Just the other day, one of the kids was swinging a plastic sword while riding his bike and he was smacking his brothers in the back of the head as he rode along. He was charging them like he'd seen in the movies. He hit one of them and about knocked him over the handlebars. You could hear it clear down the street. There was another little boy who would bite anybody around him. He'd bite you if you were holding him. He'd bite other children. He had a real bad problem there for a while, and he wasn't the only one. We had one or two others who were biters, but he was the worst one.

I used to think I had problems with my kids years ago; I had one son I used to chase around a tree like a squirrel until I got tired of chasing him. But the problems they have with the kids here make our kids seem tame. You wouldn't believe the stories behind them. Sometimes they will just get so upset about the things that have happened to them in the past that they'll sit down and start crying.

It makes you feel good, like you are really doing something to help them, when you can get through to them. For a long time, I was doing more than seventy hours a week of volunteer time. I helped put together the Intergenerational Center, and I read to kids and I work in the yards and I repair a lot of bicycles, too. If I get tired of working or being with the kids, I can come home to our apartment and shut the door and take a nap. In the early days, one of the seniors came up with a sign that had a smiley face on one side and a frown on the other. The idea was to put it on your door so the kids would know that you were available when the smiley face was showing, but not available when it was frowning. But the kids got wise and started turning them around to the smiley face and then knocking on the doors. You can't fool these kids.

Although he grew up in the rural South when segregation and racial discrimination were common, Biederman was taught to respect all races by his grandfather, whose parents had experienced racism as Jews in Germany and in this country. "My grandfather said you don't judge a man by the color of his skin, you judge him by what kind of friend he is to you. I also learned in the service that color didn't mean a thing when you were in a foxhole under fire and depending on the other guy to guard your back." Even as someone comfortable with people of other races, Biederman has found the lack of racial differences among the children at Hope Meadows to be remarkable, he said.

Last week, there was a new little girl in the neighborhood six or seven years old. She was black, and two of my Hope Meadows grandkids, who are also black, were talking to her about me being their grandpa. She was arguing with them, saying, "But he can't be your grandpa." The boys didn't get what she meant. It just hasn't registered with them that I'm white and they are black, so we can't be related. Finally, one of the boys got disgusted with her because she refused to believe him. I saw him look at her and point his finger and say, "I'm telling you for the last time, *that's* my grandpa, and I don't want to talk no more about it. I'm not going to tell you again!"

Most of the Hope kids feel the same way. We'd been here just a few months when Fran and I were standing at the jewelry counter in Wal-Mart one day and I heard someone say, "Hi, Grandpa!" and the next thing I knew Marquis Calhoun, who was about fourteen years old then, had both arms around my waist and he was hugging me and holding on. There was a black couple I didn't know standing nearby and I heard the black man say, "There ain't no way." He was looking at the little black boy and at me, an old white guy, and saying that. So I turned to him and said, "Oh, yes, there *is* a way."

Our kids are mostly black here, though we've had some Chinese and a couple Filipinos come and go, along with quite a few white kids. None of them here seem to look at color anymore. The only color they know is the color of love. They know that everyone genuinely cares for them here. It really is a lot like the place where I grew up. My grandfather's house and the country towns around it. Everybody knew everybody. Everybody watched out for everybody else. I have come home, I guess.

Chapter Ten

"THIS IS WHAT A CHILD'S LIFE IS SUPPOSED TO BE."

Elsa Raab begins her newspaper route at noon on schooldays when she puts five-year-old Marisa, the youngest of her three adopted children, into her white Nissan minivan and drives into town. At their first stop, Elsa picks up a hefty bundle of one hundred freshly printed Champaign *News-Gazettes*. A few blocks later, she drops off Marisa at the American Lutheran Church preschool. Elsa then guides the minivan out the north edge of Rantoul into the low, open arms of central Illinois. She steers with her elbows and knees while stuffing ad sections and folding the papers in her lap. "You couldn't do this in Chicago traffic, but you can in the country," the Hope Meadows mother said cheerily.

The first delivery on her 120-mile route is a farmhouse on Illinois 45 just north of town. From there, this determined, good-natured, and faith-filled woman makes a steady stop-and-go journey through the grain fields and villages of Champaign and Ford counties. Elsa completes roughly two-thirds of her route each day before breaking off to retrieve Marisa at preschool, and also nine-year-old

Steven, who has completed his day at Northview Elementary, just a block away.

As Elsa returns to the meandering blacktop, the towheaded, fair-skinned boy and the sable-haired Asian girl pitch in for the rest of the route. The kids fold *News-Gazettes* and battle over who deposits papers in the news boxes. Elsa and her children generally end the three-and-a-half-hour tour around three P.M. just as thirteen-year-old Katara gets off the junior high school bus. Their final delivery is to the Country Health Nursing Home in the village of Gifford. Elsa saves this stop for last because Marisa and Steven enjoy handing papers out to the elderly residents. Their favorite is Clay, who waits for them at the door in his wheelchair. "The kids talk to Clay and I think he is disappointed when they don't come and he has to talk to me," said Elsa, who has taken a daily chore that supplements her $20,000 annual income and transformed it into a family adventure.

"Delivering papers is very unglamorous. But with mileage, I make about $1,300 a month to help pay the bills, and it's good for the kids because we all work together, and I'm home when they are home," she said.

Elsa Raab is forty-eight years old, and certainly has other lifestyle options. She has a bachelor's degree in elementary education and psychology from Bryan College in Dayton, Tennessee, as well as a master's in computer science from DePaul University in Chicago. Two years before she moved to Hope Meadows from Chicago, 140 miles to the north, she was earning $48,000 a year as a market researcher at Searle Pharmaceuticals. She lived in a two-bedroom condo in Lake Bluff, an affluent northern suburb, and, by most measures, she had a very successful life. "I'd just gotten a promotion, I loved my job, and all was going well," she said. "But I didn't have what I most wanted in my life—children!"

For six years after I got my bachelor's degree, I taught and worked as a missionary in Mexico, North Carolina, Brazil, Suriname, and Tennessee, and ever since then I'd had a plan to adopt children one day, but it had gotten sidetracked. I'd had a relationship with a guy, but it didn't work out. Then in December of '94, I read a magazine article about a single mom who had adopted a baby from China. Up to that point, I didn't realize it was possible for a single woman to adopt. It hit me: "I could have a baby?" The magazine article provided a phone number for people interested in adopting Chinese orphans. It was at the U.S. State Department. They gave me a number to call in Chicago. I said, "I'm forty-three, can I get a baby?" They said, "Sure." I said, "I'm single, can I still get a baby?" They said, "No problem." The plan that had been in the back of my mind suddenly blossomed. Nine months later, I was on my way home from China with my beautiful six-month-old Marisa.

These children are orphaned because the Chinese government has a one-child-per-family policy. In rural areas, they are allowed to have two children if the first one is a daughter. People want to have sons who will take care of them when they grow old. The emphasis is on boys. If the second child is a girl, they often abandon them. The orphanages are full of girls. It was expensive to go to China and to adopt Marisa, but I could afford it with my job. Then I realized that I did not like being a working mom. I had a woman watching Marisa while I was at work, but I wanted to figure out a way to stay home with her. I found my answer while watching *Nightline* in October of 1996, when they did a story on Hope Meadows. I saw that and thought, "Yes! That is what I want to do. I can adopt more kids, be a stay-at-home mom, and have a whole community to help me." Still, it wasn't easy to give up my job in Chicago. My brother said I was crazy. I'd been at Searle for ten years and the benefits were really good. When I told them why I was leaving, the vice president of our division said it was the most unique reason he'd ever heard. They threw me a big party. And before I'd even moved out of my condo, Hope Meadows called with a child for me. It was Steven.

While Marisa quickly developed into an extremely bright, inquisitive dynamo of a child, Steven proved to be a complex and worrisome puzzle, which is understandable given the turmoil he experienced at a very young age. Steven was seven when he came to Elsa. He'd been born into a very large family. There was no father in the home. Several of the children had different fathers. Steven's mother, who was herself abused as a child, has been diagnosed as mentally ill with manic depression and borderline multiple personality disorder. She often left her children unsupervised. Steven still bears a scar from being burned with a clothes iron and he'd once been nearly drowned. He and his siblings were taken from their home one night in a police raid ordered by a social service agency.

Steven had been in eight different foster homes in barely seven years by the time he was sent to Hope Meadows. He was diagnosed with behavior disorders and learning disabilities. On the boy's first day of school after arriving at Hope Meadows, his teachers called Elsa and informed her that he was not capable of handling a full day of classes, so he'd been assigned to a half-day program for children with behavior disorders.

Steven's first year with Elsa and Marisa was extremely difficult. While he was never violent toward her or Marisa, he frequently went into uncontrollable fits of temper, throwing things, hiding under his bed, and running away. On his first Halloween with Elsa, Steven ran ahead of her and Marisa while trick-or-treating. He joined a pack of older boys from outside his neighborhood and was gone before Elsa could stop him. Less than fifteen minutes later, Rantoul police found him wandering the streets far from Hope Meadows. He was unhurt, but the trip home in the patrol car triggered traumatic memories of the night he'd been taken by police from his birth mother and his siblings. In the days and weeks that followed, Steven's behavior worsened. He threw things down the stairs and pounded so loudly on closet doors that the neighbors could hear it through the walls. Hope Meadows' therapists worked with him to control his rage. One taught him to pound on his pillow when he felt a tantrum coming on, or to run, or to ride his bicycle around the neighborhood to dissipate the anger. Those techniques helped. Elsa was able to get Steven through this crisis. He responded to treatment and his schoolwork began to improve dramatically. Steven has now moved from a class for children with behavioral disorders into a regular class. He still gets special help, but he appears to be thriving beyond expectations. His most recent report card was "A's and B's," Elsa said.

His ability is pretty low, according to his tests, but he is performing way above his ability. He still has trouble with language and remembering names of his classmates. When he first came to Hope he couldn't even talk. His auditory processing is not connecting well, but his math computation is up to grade level and reading computation is at grade level. The best news is he doesn't act out much anymore. He is hyperactive, but it comes out in impulsiveness. He is a very loving kid. He really cares about other people. He wants to be a real people pleaser, and he particularly loves the seniors.

At first, it was very hard with Steven's problems. I didn't know it would be this hard. I'd taught school and I'd had difficult kids, but it was nothing like this. This is the most challenging job I've ever done. When Steven was having a bad time, it was like, "Wow, is it really worth it? Did I do the right thing? Am I messing up Marisa by exposing her to this?" That's my biggest worry. Being a parent is tough, but I read a quote in *Reader's Digest* from John Irving's book *A Prayer for Owen Meany*. It said, "If you are lucky enough to find a way of life you love, you have to find the courage to live it." That's what I have been trying to do.

Elsa's third child is Katara, a sweet-faced, African-American girl, who came to her in July of 1998 at the age of ten. She had lived with an older foster parent in Chicago for five years, but that guardian had decided that she could not keep up with the sometimes vexing child as she moved into adolescence. There is no father listed on Katara's birth certificate. Her mother was a drug addict in Chicago, so as an infant, Katara was placed with an aunt. At the age of two, she left her aunt's home and was placed in foster care.

Not surprisingly, Katara came to Elsa suffering from severe depression, but so far, Elsa has had fewer problems with her than with Steven. She struggled in school, though she had no discernible learning disabilities, but once Elsa formally adopted her and Steven, Katara's behavior and her schoolwork improved greatly. She has become an avid musician, playing the flute, saxophone, violin, and drums. Katara recently came home with a report card and handed it meekly to Elsa. She had been afraid to look at it herself. Her mother examined it and discovered that Katara had made the honor roll. "It was so neat because she had never been on the honor roll before and we both got so excited."

In her first few months with Elsa, Katara established herself as a liar of considerable imagination. She constructed elaborate deceptions to mask other deceptions. Now, her mother says, she at least lies for a purpose, such as to hide the fact that she has a pile of homework to do. This poses yet another perplexing question: "With these kids, it's really hard knowing how to sort out what is normal kid behavior and what is related to their past," said Elsa. "It's also a challenge since I've been a mother only four and a half years, and I already have a teenager to deal with."

Luckily, I can rely a lot on the other parents here. They really have helped me out a lot. Michelle Roberts, another single mom who lives just across the street, has six adopted girls, including two teenagers, so she has been through a lot of similar things with her kids. Loralee Pena is a senior who was a foster child herself, and she understands Katara so well. She has dealt with the anger that comes with being abused and neglected. So, when Katara throws a tantrum and says she hates me and she wishes that I'd never adopted her, and I get all freaked out that she said horrible things to me, Loralee will tell me not to worry. She's been there. She'll say, "I said the same things when I was her age. I felt the same way."

Katara says, "Grandma Loralee understands me." She has her do her hair and they do all kinds of stuff together. Loralee was a special ed teacher, so she has helped Steven with his homework, too. Really, she's just been a gold mine for us. We see each other almost every day. The Penas really are my kids' grandparents. They kept all of their Christmas presents in their basement so they wouldn't find them, and then spent the holiday with us.

I get a lot of support here. It's a close community, and that can be a drawback in some ways. There are no secrets. For that reason, I've sought counseling outside of Hope, too. Sometimes to say what I really need to say, just to get something off my chest, it's better to go outside the community. It helps to get an outside perspective on things, too. You know, when I worked at Searle, it was very cut-and-dry. You had a work life, and you had a personal life, and the two rarely overlapped. But here, as a stay-at-home mom, my work life and my personal life are one and the same. It's like having a very large, extended family. Every senior neighbor is like an in-law. Now, that's not necessarily bad because they love the kids and they have your best interests at heart, but believe me, people at Hope Meadows aren't afraid to tell you if they think your kids shouldn't be running around barefoot. I'm not really complaining because that concern also works in my favor. I had a sinus headache one morning recently, so I missed a parent meeting. It seemed like the whole neighborhood knew within minutes. Right away, a neighbor called to make sure I was okay, and one of the seniors came over and took my kids for two hours so I could get some rest. Believe me, at Hope Meadows, I never had to worry about what to do with my kids if something comes up.

When I lived in a condo in the Chicago area I didn't even know my neighbors' names. I'd ride up the elevator with them and we didn't speak. It is so incredibly different here. I do feel like I'm part of a community now. And although being a single parent is harder than I thought it would be and busier than I thought it would be—I actually envisioned myself having time to read a lot of books—it's very rewarding to have these kids. They are so open and so sensitive. You can't hide anything from them, and they make you look at the world in a totally different way.

Now, I live for what I call "golden moments." A few days ago we went to a social skills group for five- through seven-year-olds at the Intergenerational Center. It was a great resource with a counselor who is working on her Ph.D. I was sitting there talking about it to Katara and her friends, Shannon and Elizabeth, when Steven ran into something and cut his leg. He had this big scratch and it was starting to swell. Katara ran to him and said, "I'll take you home and take care of you,

Steven." She started walking him down the street, holding his hand. Marisa ran up to them and grabbed Steven's other hand, and I thought, "This is one of those moments where it is all worthwhile." It was one of those times when it all came together. This is what a child's life is supposed to be.

When I was at Searle trying to decide what to do with my life, I asked myself whether I wanted to keep on working or whether I wanted to make a difference in someone's life. This is what I want. I want to be here. Now, when I stand back and look at my kids, I think, "Wow, someday I am going to have lots of grandkids and they will be all different races." And I wonder what they'll look like and how they'll come to see me and care for me when I'm old.

And I think, "I will be very happy with how I've spent my life."

Chapter Eleven

"I FEEL LIKE I FIT IN HERE."

As a child, Loralee Pena once told a friend that while she didn't know anything about her mother and father, she did know that she was born in Kankakee. It said so on a birth certificate that her foster mother had shown her. "The person said I must have been born in the nuthouse," Pena recalled. She ran to her foster mother with that hurtful comment, and her foster mother consoled her by saying there were several hospitals in Kankakee—not just the state mental hospital—and she was probably born in one of them.

Years later, as an adult, Loralee saw *The Hiding Place*, a movie based on the life of Corrie Ten Boom, a Dutch woman who was imprisoned in a Nazi concentration camp for hiding Jews in her home during World War II. The movie was an inspiring one of courage and spiritual strength, which Loralee found comforting, but there was something about the scenes of the prison camp that struck her as familiar and disconcerting. The prison's stark interior walls, in particular, seemed to trigger some sort of deep aching memory, as did the entrance to the camp, which was marked by a wrought-iron archway over stone columns.

Those images haunted Loralee for several days after she'd seen the movie, to the point that she asked her husband, Al, to accompany her on a trip to the town in which she'd been told she was born. Kankakee was about sixty miles north, straight up Interstate 57 from Urbana, where the Penas then lived. They drove there and found the grounds of the Kankakee Mental Health Center, which today provides care and treatment for the developmentally disabled. Most of the center's buildings were brick, but there was an older, historic landmark section of gray limestone that was part of the original campus for the Illinois Eastern Hospital for the Insane, established in 1877. "We drove around until we found that older section, then we parked and went in," Loralee said.

A person inside asked if he could help us. I told him that I was interested in seeing where the old infirmary for the mental hospital would have been in 1941, because I suspected that I might have been born there. "You are standing in it," he said.

We spent some time looking around and we went into one room that was just like in the movie with the stark walls. It seemed familiar to me. I asked the man if he had records of people who had been in the mental institution and he said he did. When I was in my twenties, I'd gone to the agency that had placed me with my foster mother and I asked to see my records. Most of the information was crossed out, but I was able to get my mother's name. It was Virginia. I told this to the man and gave him my maiden name, and he looked it up in the file. He said my mother had been a patient there, but he told me if I wanted any more information, I'd have to call and get it from the main office because he wasn't allowed to give any more out.

Before we left, I asked him if there was another entrance to the old mental hospital, one with a wrought-iron gate, and he said yes, that it was down the road and overgrown with weeds. We checked it out and that's what I'd pictured in my mind. I was two and a half months old when I was taken from that place as a ward of the state. A minister who counseled me for a few years said that the images must have been imprinted in my mind because of the trauma I went through, being rejected by my mother and taken from her. There weren't any words attached to that time in my life, but when I saw the similar images in the movie, it jarred the memories from my earliest days.

I have taken some psych courses over the years and they are finding that people have memories even of things they heard inside their mother's womb. My memories were still there, because thirty-seven years later, I was still dealing with who I am and what earthly good I am. As a teacher, I was fine, but I wasn't a great wife or mother because I didn't know what those were. I had never really bonded with my foster mother. I always had the sense that someday my own mother would come back for me.

Loralee Pena, now fifty-nine years old, is olive-skinned, dark-haired, and gracious, but with a melancholy that lingers over her even when she smiles. It is a trait common to children and adults who have spent long periods of their lives feeling unwanted and apart. It takes years of healing to overcome those emotional wounds. "I'm still something of a mixed-up foster kid at fifty-nine," she said.

For most of her adult life, she has attempted to heal by tracing her parentage and by trying to understand why she was unloved. She has uncovered fragments of information here and there in old files, in the memories of strangers, and in the musty old wing of the former Kankakee mental hospital:

Loralee's birth mother was orphaned at the age of three when her own parents were killed in an automobile accident. Her guardians were elderly and they sent her to a Seventh Day Adventist girls' school in St. Louis. She later married a Midwestern optometrist who divorced her because of her mental illness. She was a severe manic-depressive who refused to care for Loralee after she was born in the mental health center's infirmary. Her father was listed as unknown, but Loralee's own research has led her to conclude that he was an Hispanic man with whom her mother had a brief affair during a visit to an aunt in Texas. "That aunt tried to adopt me, but they told her she was too old," Loralee said.

Her mother died of pneumonia in 1962. In examining her mother's death records, Loralee noted that a daughter had claimed her body. Loralee then realized that she must have had a sister or at least a half-sister. Several years ago Loralee's own daughter contacted the woman listed on the death certificate. "She told my daughter that she'd been warned that her mother's other children might contact her, but she said she didn't want to know them," Loralee said sadly.

As an infant, Loralee was given a permanent home, but she really never had a sense of family there. She was placed as a foster child with a fifty-year-old widowed teacher in Urbana. They lived with her foster mother's sister, father, and five other foster children. It was a big and turbulent household. Loralee developed an early bond with her foster grandfather who often took her on his daily walks. "When we'd go walking, my foster mother would always say, 'Now don't lose Grandpa.'" But one day, when she was two years old, her grandfather was simply gone from the household without explanation. Eleven years later, she learned that he had committed suicide. She has come to believe that she must have heard the gunshot because his bedroom was next to hers, and, for as long as she can remember, she has been terrified by loud, banging sounds.

Loralee was never adopted by her foster mother. She grew up feeling like an unwanted visitor. She was always introduced as "the girl who lives with us." Other children called her "nigger" because her skin was darker than most of her foster siblings, and they made fun of the fact that she had no father.

The one bright area in her life was her performance in school, where she drove herself to "prove I had some worth." She made the National Honor Society in high school, and her foster care caseworker was so impressed that she helped Loralee get a state scholarship to the University of Illinois. She graduated with a degree in special education in 1963.

She was twenty-four years old when she met Al Pena on a bus from Champaign to Rantoul. She was working as a special ed teacher at the school for servicemen's children on the Chanute Field Air Force Base. Al, a native of Victoria, Texas, was thirty-seven and stationed at Chanute as a medical technician. "My foster mom had always told me not to date anybody from the base, but Al asked me to go to coffee and I knew the police station was right across from the coffee shop, so I felt safe," Loralee recalled.

She'd long felt that her father was Hispanic, so she has come to view her marriage to an older, Mexican-American as another step in her lifelong search for family. In spite of her often difficult struggles with identity and self-acceptance, Loralee has been an outstanding teacher, mother, and grandmother. Her daughter, Marcella, who is an elementary school teacher, is married with two children, and lives in Urbana. With their own grandchildren less than forty miles away, the Penas could have easily limited their caregiving to family members at this stage in their lives, but they chose to live in

Hope Meadows because Loralee sensed it would help her in coming "full circle."

I feel like I fit in here because the children, and even many of the adults, have come from similar backgrounds. I will say that sometimes it is hard for me, especially when the kids here get adopted and they have adoption parties for them. I've not gone to most of them. I just couldn't go because I still feel hurt that my foster mother never adopted me. That was always an issue for me with her and I resented her when I got older. I always felt like I was in limbo as her foster child. I acted out against her because of that. I had a lot of anger and I did hurtful things to her. It is also difficult for me if kids don't make it here. We've had some who just didn't work—their needs were too great, or they were a bad fit for families or, as in the case of one boy, they had to be institutionalized. It bothers me a great deal to see that.

All in all, Hope has been a reality check for me. In these children I see the same behavior that I once exhibited. When Katara Raab tells Elsa that she doesn't want her to be her mother anymore, I understand that anger she is expressing. I tell Elsa not to personalize it because it's not about her; it's about Katara's feelings of being an outsider, especially since she is black and has a white mom. It's actually a compliment to Elsa that Katara is secure enough with her that she feels safe to express those feelings.

When you care for people like Katara and me, you get scars because we lash out. Al has them. He has been very patient and understanding at my venting over the years. My foster mother had scars, too. I was an angry little being. My foster mother once said that the more she did for me, the uglier my actions became. There is just so much anger and rejection to deal with. Fortunately, kids here have the opportunity to be counseled and nurtured and not feel different because so many of the children here are from similar circumstances. They aren't different here. They understand each other.

I talk with Katara a lot and I tell her how I would tear up my room in anger, too. She can talk to me about what she's feeling, because she knows I've been there. Often it is easier for these children to take advice from someone outside their adoptive family members. I feel good about having the opportunity to do that for them.

I really have come full circle, and I think I'll be here until the last deck chair slides overboard. This is a good place for me to end up. I've given up hope at times in my life, and the Lord has given it back and showed me that there is a reason for me to be here. I can keep other children from losing hope because I know what they feel like. This is a place where I can fit in, and where they can fit in, and get into the flow of life again. After the life I've had, it makes sense for me to end up in a place called Hope.

Chapter Twelve

"THERE IS A LOT OF REAL CHICKEN SOUP AROUND HERE."

The Buttittas were a big family in a small town. John, a house painter, and Esther, a teacher, had four sons and three daughters. But this wasn't what brought them to prominence in Thomasboro, a central Illinois farm village of about 1,200 residents. It was their work in the community. John was a school board member and he watched the skies for trouble over Thomasboro as the town's Emergency Services and Disaster Agency coordinator. He was also active in the local Catholic parish and always available as a volunteer to paint this, haul that, or raise money for a worthy cause. Esther served on the village board, ran their church Sunday school program, and organized the community's first day care center, along with her work at the elementary school and at home among her children.

The Buttitta children were always being pressed into service to do what they called "gratis work" as they grew up. "It was unending," recalled Fred, now forty-four. "It seemed like we were always doing something for somebody because Dad wanted us to do it. Back then we didn't really want to do it. But looking back, it was a pretty good way to go."

Their family philosophy held that, "The Lord put us on this Earth to spread his bounty and you are supposed to use your talents, not hide them," Esther said. "We felt the more we did for others, the more we would get in return, and that is how John and I lived, and our children did, too."

John Buttitta was a giving man, and also a tough one. After doctors told him he probably had only about three months to live because of cancer, he declined chemotherapy. Instead, he went on a macrobiotic diet and, after two years, he was doing so well that he returned to working part-time. He and Esther also dared to make plans again. They were looking forward to her retirement from teaching after twenty-four years, so they could do more things together. Typically, they did not intend to retire to a beach or golf course community. Their dream was to move out West and do volunteer work, perhaps teaching needy children among the Native American families on reservations there.

Sadly, that was not to be. John was killed in a car crash in Champaign in 1987. He and Esther had been married nearly forty years. Her husband's death left her grieving and feeling thrown off course. "I had been looking forward to retirement with him; I could hardly wait. And then he died, and my plans changed."

She went ahead and retired from teaching and embarked on a "hard" ten-year journey in search of her place in the world as a solitary woman with grown children. She spent time at the homes of several of her children, but realized that they were fully engaged in their own lives.

When I was staying with my daughter in Phoenix for two months, we went through all the retirement places around there, and they all seemed so sterile. I don't think I could ever live in a retirement home because, for one thing, the mortality rates are so high. And I don't like the idea of going into a retirement or nursing home and letting everybody do everything for me. I think you lose your will to live when you do that. I think we all have a purpose and you just need to keep going.

Esther told her parish priest in Thomasboro that she wanted to continue serving others and he referred her to the Catholic Workers organization, which was founded in 1933 by Dorothy Day and Peter Maurin. Catholic Workers volunteers operate homeless shelters around the country. Esther chose to volunteer at the Jean Donovan Catholic Worker House in St. Cloud, Minnesota, a shelter for homeless men and women. She moved into the old yellow brick farmhouse and quickly realized that one part of the Catholic Workers philosophy ran counter to her personal preferences—"living in poverty."

I was accustomed to an air-conditioned house and an air-conditioned car. In St. Cloud, I had a room with no air-conditioning, broken windows, no curtains, no shades, a lot of dirt, bats that flew through the transom, and a half-bath with no toilet seat. I don't think the house had ever been cleaned. So, I cleaned it. It had once been a beautiful house owned by a wealthy farmer. It had a music room, a library, a butler's pantry, and a narrow back stairway for the help. There were five bedrooms upstairs and a laundry facility and a screened-in room. I was the only staff member on the second floor. The others lived on the third, which was even hotter.

I lived there for a year and I learned a lot about the homeless. People who have nothing go crazy when something of theirs is disturbed.

One fellow accused another of stealing his razor and he called the police. Another called the police when someone stole one of his two eggs. They were always being "rolled" by muggers outside the house. There is a vicious cycle to homelessness. They'd become destitute and come stay with us and try to recover. They could eat well and sleep better and get their lives under control and find a job. But often, they'd work for a while and then they'd get sick, or something would happen, and they'd have nothing to fall back on, so they'd become destitute again.

After completing her one-year term as a volunteer staff member at the Jean Donovan House, Esther decided to continue her work closer to her children and grandchildren in Illinois. She moved into an apartment at Clare House, a homeless shelter in Bloomington. She worked there and in an affiliated soup kitchen called Loaves and Fishes. Her life improved there, and not simply because her new apartment was air-conditioned. She was closer to her children and grandchildren—one son lived in town—and she found companionship in a group for senior single women. "I have a lot of family but they are busy with life. This group had people with time for me. We went on bus trips and went out together. I still see some of them. They are wonderful people."

After two years working with families and the homeless at Clare House, Esther felt she needed more time for herself. She rented a small apartment back in Thomasboro, and called the school superintendent. "I told him I was back, and he said, 'Good. I have two pregnant teachers.' So I taught for a year while the teachers took maternity leave." At the end of the school year, her son in Bloomington called Esther for help. His marriage had broken up and he needed her help with his children. "I went to take care of them and they ended up caring for me," she noted.

Esther's determination to remain active and of service was thwarted by her own faltering health in the years after John's death. While with her son in Bloomington, she underwent two hip replacement surgeries, and back surgery, only to then be stricken with chest pains that led to a heart bypass operation.

She was recuperating from the cardiac surgery when she read a newspaper story about Hope Meadows. She was seventy years old and though she had to use a walker to get around, she was not yet willing to give up her active lifestyle.

I saw the newspaper story, and I thought, "That's something I can do." I called them and said I thought I had something to offer, and they told me to come in for an interview. I came in and told them I'd been a teacher and I raised seven children so I thought I could be of help. I moved in three years ago and, yes, I love living here.

Hope is not a cure for loneliness, but it is a sustaining force. It is love. When you give love here, it comes back to you. It happens around here all the time. One of my friends here, Eleene, fell several months ago and broke her shoulder. The entire neighborhood rallied around her. She now has a plastic shoulder joint but her doctors tell her she is doing remarkably well, and she credits her quick recovery to the kids and the community.

There is a lot of chicken soup going around here. I'm not talking about the *Chicken Soup* books. I'm talking about the real thing. I came home yesterday from tutoring children for an hour and a half at the Intergenerational Center and my neighbor, Bill Biederman, stuck his head out the door and said, "We had chicken soup for supper, do you want a bowl?" That happens *all* the time. It's just a wonderful feeling. Somebody is always calling or stopping by and saying they are cooking out, "C'mon over," or inviting you just to come and talk.

When I first moved in, I sat in a lawn chair out front in the yard and the children would just come by and start talking to me. We built up rapport right away. When something is bothering them, they'll just come and sit and talk to you because they feel the foster grandparents are safe. They seem to know that you will love them no matter what, and that is just a great feeling.

Esther has short gray hair, bright red eyeglass frames, and a go-getter's spirit. She has earned a reputation as a skilled seamstress at Hope Meadows, where she has made several elaborate "Daisy Kingdom" party dresses for neighborhood children. Her apartment is carefully decorated and tidy except for the designated "messy room" where she sews. That room, she discovered, is a comfort to the children who come calling. "One of the little girls couldn't get over how neat my place was, so I took her up to the messy room and she was thrilled that it was messier than her own," she said.

Working with Hope children is a slow process of discovery, according to Esther, whose teaching experience helped prepare her for the challenges offered by troubled, uprooted young people.

When I first started tutoring here, there were kids who would stand in a corner and face the wall rather than talk to me. It can be difficult because we don't have information on their histories. Only the parents get that. So, we don't always know how to handle individual children.

We have to just take them as they come to us, and we run with them any way we can. You have to build trust. It's a wonderful feeling to do that. I've seen many great changes in these kids since I've been here. Now, one of those children who would stand in the corner comes and rings my doorbell and says, "Hi, Grandma! How are you!"

I guess I love it here because there is something to get up for every morning. I like watching children develop. I like to feel like I'm helping with that. And I like that people honestly care about how you feel and about your well-being. It's meant a healthier life for me. No matter how much I hurt, I still get up and go because I know the children are waiting for me. If I get despondent or worried about something, there is always some sort of pat on the arm. One little girl I was tutoring looked up at me the other day and said, "Why are you so grouchy?" She was right. I hadn't been feeling very well that day, but she made me laugh, so I wasn't grouchy anymore.

Because of my back problems, I can't pick up the little ones and do some of the things I'd like to do anymore, but I love to hug them. I don't even have to ask them for hugs anymore. They'll run up and knock you down with hugs. I tell them that a hug is like gasoline to a car. It keeps me going.

This is really the best place for me now. I love seeing children go through stages of development, helping them wherever I can. One of the girls I was asked to tutor used to come to our sessions and just flounce around and complain about her mother. She's a teenager and it was just her age. She'd talk to me and I provided a release for all the things she was feeling. I saw her two times a week for a half-hour and her grades started to come up. She began to feel better about herself and about being a teenager. She'd been through a lot and I don't know what would have happened to her without this place. Now she comes to my apartment and talks to me all the time. She'll talk for forty-five minutes about boys, cars, sports, and her family. I just listen. I love it. I love to see how she is handling her relationships. She is doing such a good job, getting rounded out as a person.

One day, she asked me to chaperon her sixteenth birthday party and it just floored me. She wanted me to be there. There's a saying that when you give to others, you get twice as much in return. Well, here I get twice as much as I give. I just get that real pleased feeling deep down inside that I've done something correctly. Something has worked. It's love. Love makes it all go round.

> Esther has come to enjoy life at Hope Meadows so much that she recruited her grown son to live there also. Fred Buttitta had just gone through a divorce in which he shares custody of his six-year-old son. At Esther's suggestion, he moved into a Hope Meadows apartment under a provision that allows ten percent of the community's housing to be occupied by nonadoptive parents who are willing to fill a need. Now, he, too, is giving time to Hope kids, with his own boy in tow.

After my divorce, I was looking for a place to live and my mother thought this would be a good transition place for me. She's the kind of person who, when she has something that she thinks is good, she likes to share it. I'm feeling comfortable here now and it's a very good environment for my son who lives with me. I let him go out in the yard the other day and when I looked out there were three kids pushing on the seat of his pants trying to help him get up a tree. This is really a neighborhood like the one I had growing up. Everybody watches out for everybody.

Chapter Thirteen

"SOME KIDS ARE SURVIVORS."*

Susan Washburn could not find a job in her field of sports adminis-
tration after graduating from college in Indiana and marrying her
boyfriend, Rob. So, she took a job as a teacher's assistant at the
Cunningham's Children's Home, a private foster care residential program in Urbana. There, she learned that she'd led "a sheltered life."

There were kids in high school that you knew didn't follow the
rules, but I'd never seen violent, raging children. The kids at Cunningham's could be very sweet to you but many had a really bad side, too. At
the drop of a pin, they could change totally and start yelling and cursing
at you. I worked with children with behavioral problems. Initially I was
assigned to monitor one particular child, but I ended up working also
with the ten to twelve kids in the classroom. I had to keep an eye on one
of the kids, though, because he was threatening to me. He was a huge
twelve-year-old. I had never been physically intimidated by anyone

*Note: The family in this story no longer lives at Hope Meadows. They asked that their
names be changed to protect their privacy.

until this boy. He was like a thug. I'd catch him doing things that I had to report and he'd get in trouble.

Once he picked up a chair and acted like he was going to hit me on top of the head. I knew he probably wouldn't do it because he had never gotten violent before; he'd only threatened it. He didn't follow through, but it scared me. Most of the kids at Cunningham's are in the foster care system but they are not likely to get adopted because foster families can't handle them. It's for the most severe children. Often they are medicated. They can be violent. The environment was so intense. I didn't feel like I was really helping the kids a whole lot. I learned that children really develop their personalities under the age of five and Cunningham's only took kids that were six and older. So, for the most part, their characters were already formed. I decided that I wanted to be able to help kids before they got to the point of those at Cunningham's. I wanted to help children without parents have better lives than that. I also wanted to do something with my life that I thought was important.

The job at Cunningham's wasn't enough. I felt that kids needed somebody there for them all the time. I had never thought about having children, even my own, at that point. We were content with our lives; we were still in our twenties. But it just hit me. I kept seeing more and more of them coming into Cunningham's and I thought maybe I could do something to prevent kids from being shuffled around. We'd heard about Hope Meadows and Rob's mother, who had once thought about doing foster care, reminded us of it, so we checked it out.

Rob and Susan were quite mature for such a young couple, but their goals differed at that point. Rob, who grew up on his family's farm, was focused on his career, and on building a foundation for their future. The couple had already purchased their first home, an older residence in Champaign, that they'd renovated. Adopting children, or taking in foster children, had never occurred to him. Rob noted, "When Susan told me she wanted to get involved in foster care, I had little or no interest."

She had a deep desire to do something like this, and I said okay, but I made it clear that it was not my life's goal. I didn't have the same need that she felt. I told her at the time that I could probably do it for her, but I wasn't real sure about adopting a child. I told her we both had to agree on the child, that we had to feel like we loved the child as our own son or daughter.

The way I looked at it was that it was something my wife wanted to do and it didn't interrupt my goals. While some of the families are drawn to Hope Meadows by the financial aspects of it, we are not as tied to that. I would say that with the income they pay for one parent to be a full-time care provider, and with the free housing, no real estate taxes, maintenance, and other benefits, it's probably a value of $40,000 a year for us to live here. But I can tell you that people who want to take in foster kids shouldn't do it to increase cash flow. Believe me, it is more beneficial to be here than in regular foster care, but it's not something you do to build wealth.

The Washburns were the youngest, and only childless, couple when they moved into a Hope Meadows home in July of 1996. Susan was twenty-six and eager to take in a child, though she and her husband had given careful consideration to just what sort of child they would allow into their home. Susan's experiences with violent and threatening adolescents made her determined not to accept older children. They were also reluctant to take in a newborn, since neither of them had experience in caring for infants. They decided that they preferred to start with a child in the two- to five-year-old range, but to their frustration, none were available in their first four months at Hope Meadows.

They offered us ten to fifteen different children, but after looking into each of their backgrounds, I said no. One of them was sixteen years old; I was only twenty-six myself. Another boy was ten and almost as tall as I was. He had kicked or hit a teacher, so I said no to him. I didn't want to be home alone with a boy who had done that. We wanted a toddler and they didn't have any for us. They offered us a sibling group of four and I considered it, but Rob thought it was too much. One of the children was in a wheelchair. We had no experience in dealing with children in that situation. The staff people were wondering what we were doing here because we'd turned down so many children, but we reminded them that from the beginning interviews we'd said we wanted toddlers only.

Matching needy children to adoptive families is an inexact science, even within Hope Meadows, where parents generally are willing to accept considerable risk in caring for some of the most traumatized young people in the foster care system. Sometimes the best intentions are thwarted, not by a child's needs, but because of a family's. When that happens, the results can be heartbreaking for everyone involved. It is also true, however, that when the chemistry is right between a child and his adoptive family, other issues and challenges often can be overcome. The Washburns have experienced both sides.

The quiet six-year-old boy named David did not exactly match the Washburns' cautious parameters, but he quickly won them over. The foster child had been living with another Hope Meadows family, but they had already adopted another boy of nearly the same age. It was decided that the two of them needed more attention than that family could provide. "I'd met him and although, at six and a half, he was a little older than we'd wanted, I liked the fact that he was shy and quiet. I thought I could work with him better than with an outrageously hyperactive child. He is also such a cute little boy," Susan said.

David was given up by his birth mother when he was one month old. She was a teenaged mother, who'd already given up two children to the state's Department of Children and Family Services. David was moved from one temporary foster care home to the next before he was placed with his two half-siblings at a foster home in Rantoul. He lived there for two years under the guardianship of a single foster mother before DCFS removed all of the children. The half-siblings were returned to the birth mother but she had terminated her parental rights for David, so he was sent to Hope Meadows.

Somewhere in his egregious journey through the child welfare system, David had been seriously traumatized. There were disturbing reports about things that he'd seen and been exposed to. When they first took over guardianship of David, the Washburns were most apprehensive about his treatment with Ritalin, the increasingly controversial drug used to control hyperactive behavior in children. "My concern was that we were considering adopting this child, whose school was saying that he needed to be on this drug so he would be under control," said Rob.

The Department of Children and Family Services had diagnosed him with attention-deficit disorder, and put him on Ritalin. The school he attended in Rantoul was adamant that he be kept on the drug. They said he would be climbing the walls without it, but we argued that he didn't behave that way at home. We went to a neurologist but he kept saying, "If the school feels he needs to be on Ritalin then he should be on it." We said, "Who is the doctor here?"

Susan did a lot of research. She found that kids with ADHD [attention-deficit hyperactivity disorder] can't turn it on and off. You are either ADHD or you are not. We were going to a church at the time that had an hour-and-a-half Sunday service, and David could sit through the entire service without any problems. We felt that his problems at school were more related to the turmoil that he'd experienced in his life. We were willing to bend over backwards to get him off Ritalin. Susan volunteered to be in the classroom with him, but the school thought she just wanted to check up on the teacher. We had no qualms about the teacher.

We finally went to the head of the DCFS. I think we are the only people ever to ask that a foster child be taken off Ritalin. Most want children to go on it. We waited until school was out and kept him off it all summer. He was fine. Then we had him examined and they decided he was not ADHD after all. We put him in a different school and he has had no problems.

With David, at this point, the biggest long-term problem we see is that he is black and we are white. We have some concern that it could become a problem for him when he becomes a teenager, particularly if he feels troubled about being rejected by his birth mother. He could go through a huge rebellion at fourteen or fifteen. It's normal with teenagers anyway, but when you mix in the other factors, along with being adopted, it's something you have to think about. We tell him that we can't control what happened to him in the first six years of his life because we weren't with him, but we are with him now and we will work with him to fix his pattern of behavior. My focus will be to keep David as close as possible so that when those issues and emotions come up, we can deal with them. I am not sure exactly how we'll do that, but we'll try.

I've had people say that we could be in for a lot of trouble as he grows up. I was raised in a little town with all white people. I go back home and people say they think it's great that we've adopted a black child, but you know they are thinking, "What are you doing?" I'm not necessarily someone who values others' opinions. I do my own thing. I won't let anybody else's ignorance or evil dictate my actions. But I can tell some people question the choices we have made.

If you'd have told me five or six years ago that I was going to adopt a child, I would have said you were nuts. I don't care about the fact that he is black. I've said to David that he can let the racial difference make him weaker or stronger. We've talked about the fact that it may be an issue for him someday. It's a lot to put on a child at six, but we want to communicate with him. It really has not been an issue in the family. Our parents and siblings have been great. David has a great personality. He's a little ornery, which I like. I look at David and I see him as my son. I see him say and do some of the same things that I say and do. I see myself in him.

Their overall good experience with David encouraged the couple to seek another needy child. Two months after David joined the family, they took in a brown-haired, two-year-old girl who had been in both foster care and under the guardianship of family members. But the child's situation was difficult to deal with because she still had ties to her former foster mother, her birth grandmother, and her birth mother, Susan said.

There were so many people coming in and out of her life that she called four different women "Mother." I felt like her full-time baby-sitter, because she'd spend weekends with her birth grandmother and her birth mother had her several days a week, and then there was a former foster mother who loved her, too. There were so many adults trying to make decisions in this child's life. It was very difficult for us. When she was with us, it was like she was our child, but there were all these visits from her birth mom, and calls from her caseworkers and her former foster parents, and other people got involved.

I really felt that it was not working the way I'd hope it would, and after eleven months with us, she went back to her own family, and it was for the better. It was hard to see her go because I worried what she was thinking about being moved again. You don't know how much a three-year-old understands. There were too many people involved in her life, and it taught me a lesson about taking children with so many ties to other people.

Shortly after the girl was returned to her family's care, Susan became pregnant. Even then she wanted to take in another child immediately if one could be found because "I knew we were capable of providing a home for another child if we could find one we could work with." When they could not find a suitable match right away, they decided to postpone it until their own son was born. Nine months after the birth of Joshua, they agreed to serve as guardians and to consider adopting Brad, a five-year-old African-American boy who had been in the foster care system since the age of one month.

Brad's mother gave up her parental rights just after he was born. Although he had no discernible health or behavioral problems, he had been in at least four foster homes before coming to Hope Meadows. Susan was drawn to him in part because his birth mother was no longer involved in his life. "It's easier on our family that way," she said. "I ran into David's birth mother in the store one day. We haven't had much contact with her other than she's asked for his school pictures. She had her other two children with her. She asked

David for a hug, and when he hugged her, she looked at me, and we both had to turn away. It made tears well up in my eyes. I've heard of other biological parents who stalk their children when they are adopted or go into foster care. She did not overstep her bounds. She just asked how he was doing. I'm thankful that she understands that she gave him up and that we can offer what is best for him now. I'm sure it's not easy, and that's why we liked it that Brad's mother was not involved in his life."

Brad's arrival so soon after the birth of the couple's first child did not make for an easy assimilation. Rob saw Brad competing with Joshua, his natural child, for Susan's attentions, and it triggered a resentment that both alarmed and distressed him. "I didn't know there was going to be this disparity of affection," he said. After months of reflection, and no little anguish, Rob decided that they should not, and would not adopt Brad, even though that is what he and Susan initially intended to do. Even though Susan wants to adopt him. Even though, Rob admits, Brad is "a good little boy who doesn't pose any obvious risks."

Before we had Joshua, I was afraid that I would feel differently about David, who we adopted before Joshua was born, but I haven't experienced that. I have a bond with David. I have a sense of guilt about Brad because he is such a good kid, but by the same token, I look at him and . . . when Joshua and David smile, it makes me feel good inside. When Brad does, it doesn't do anything. It doesn't register. I'm not a person who makes decisions based on emotion, but it's like marrying somebody—that feeling has to be there.

Quite frankly, I'm a pretty cocky guy, but I don't think as highly of myself as I once did because of this. I wish I could say that I love Brad, but those feelings don't come. I think if we hadn't had Joshua, who is our first natural child, it might be different. I somehow see Brad, and this may sound terrible, too, I see him interfering with my experience of having a child naturally, because Brad needs a mom and dad, too, but when he takes our time away from Joshua, I have these bad emotions. They come and I can't help feeling them. I resent him when he and Joshua compete for Susan's attentions. Even though it is not his fault, that is the emotion that goes through me.

It is important for me to be close to my children, and sometimes I think I could fake it, but I'm not sure if I'll be able to do that. So, we have decided not to adopt him. My wife wants to, but I have decided not to, based on the fact that emotionally I am not there. Even though he is probably the perfect foster child with no behavioral disorders. He gets good grades in school—he got outstanding grades in kindergarten. He does what he is told. He is just a good kid. But as I told Brenda and Susan, now that we have had a baby of our own, it would be harder for me to adopt.

Susan and I have discussed this at length and she has had some tears, and some words with me, but I am just not there with him. I do want him to stay at Hope because he is familiar with the surroundings and the families here. We are still looking for a family for him. There was a couple who turned him down, so now we are looking at other families. One is a single parent. She is a good lady, but I think he needs a father, and although I don't have control of the situation, I would like to make sure he has the best. I really hope he stays with a family here. I don't know how David will respond to his leaving. I've been trying to think of what I am going to say to him . . .

I told one of the social workers at Hope that I look at it like this: Five years from now, I would rather be in a position where I regret not adopting him, rather than in one where I regret that I did adopt him. My primary responsibility is to my family and my interaction with the family, and it may sound harsh, but that comes first and that is where I'm at on this. With a child like Brad, a child who has no problems, there should be no trouble getting him adopted by someone else, hopefully. I pray that there won't be.

> Because of Rob's resistance to adopting Brad or any more children from the foster care system, he and Susan decided to move out of Hope Meadows with David and Joshua. They have provided a permanent home and family to one child who might never have known them, and they want to make room for another family that might do the same. "I wish I would have helped one more child, but it's an issue with my husband and, being married, you can't push that if it is going to cause stress on the marriage," said Susan.

We won't take in any more foster children because I don't want to have to risk making them go to another home. I won't take that chance. It has been too difficult to tell Brad that he has to go to another home. With David, it was an easy fit. We worked hard on the Ritalin issue with him, but socially, he clicks with my husband. He has a great personality and he gets along with everybody and he has a great sense of humor and all these other qualities. He is very personable and does so well with Joshua. It's like he's always been our son. He fits in. He is part of our family forever. I only wish I could have gotten him when he was even younger so that he would not have had the experiences that may affect him negatively later. You don't know how a child will turn out.

Some kids are survivors and that is what David is. I know David will have some struggles. I know having white parents will bring questions. We already have some kids asking about that and teasing him. But my husband is working hard to be a good father and to be close to him as a male role model.

It will be hard for David to see Brad go because he doesn't understand, and you can't really explain the real reasons. We will have to focus on making sure he is not affected too strongly. Brad was an excellent child for us. Rob said he would have to be in the top ten percent of foster children. It's amazing how good he has been. Foster children often have horrendous behaviors. You would be shocked at some of the things they do. I feel bad, but I try to frame it as a better situation for Brad in the long run.

I'm trying not to think about Brad leaving. I get very emotional at times, especially when I picture his face when we told him he wouldn't be living with us anymore. I didn't want to do it. It wasn't my decision. I have to go along with it for my husband's sake. We had to do it yesterday, tell him, and it was the worst thing I could have done to a child. There are worse things that others do, I know that, but that's the worst I'll ever have to do.

It was very emotional. To look at a child after you have just had to tell him that he is going to go live with somebody else . . . He sort of sank into himself, and his face saddened a little bit. I wonder what he was thinking. He has been such a good child. He has tried. He wanted to be good. It is his nature. I don't want him to think he is moving because he did something wrong. Even though you tell him he is a good child, he will still think that sometimes. I know what David went through when he had to leave another family and come to us. You really can't tell a child . . . you can't tell him the specifics. You can't say that Rob, emotionally, can't feel like he can be your father. You can't tell that to a small child.

When we told him, Brad didn't say anything at first. I said, "You are probably wondering why and you might feel sad." I told him that he is a very good boy. I said the person who is going to take him in—she is a neighbor—she thinks you are very good and her children have all lived other places and they are a family now and she is their mom and helps them with their school and reads them books. She wants to do it for you, too.

I tried to promote the positive, but I started crying. Then he did, too. And then my husband went next door and got the woman who is going to take him, and she had a surprise for Brad, and the present gave him something to occupy his mind. Later, we went swimming with her family and that evening we spent more time with them so he could see us with her family and know that we are friends. He will probably move over there within the next month. We are building a house and it won't be ready until August.

He seems to be adjusting to the situation and today he was wondering when he would move in. He seems to feel comfortable there. This neighbor has a little girl close to his age, so they should get along. I think we'll have another hard day when we actually move his stuff over. He is going over there a couple nights this week and he will spend Saturday night there. That might be a little hard for him. He is a very timid, introverted child most of the time. I think in the long run, it will be just fine. I just hope everything works out with his new family. I hate to see him have to make another move. He turns seven in September and the older you get, the less chance you are going to find a family to take you in, and the more likely you are to have problems, although he doesn't have any now.

He told me last night that he will miss me. Rather than say he loves me, like he always does, he said he will miss me.

Chapter Fourteen

"THIS JOB IS NEVER GOING TO END."

DEBBIE CALHOUN'S TEN THINGS KIDS NEED WHEN THEY COME TO HOPE MEADOWS

1. **Understanding:** As their parents and guardians, we need to understand who they are, where they are coming from, their feelings, the reasons behind the things they say and do.

2. **Trust:** These kids need to learn to trust us and believe in us as people they can trust. We have to prove our trustworthiness to them.

3. **Love:** Our kids must know that just because things happen that might upset us or get them in trouble, they are always loved, no matter what. They must understand that the minute they walk in the door, they are loved. They need to know that just because they do something wrong, they aren't going to be sent away again. Here, they can make mistakes.

4. **Compassion:** To learn to be compassionate toward others, kids have to experience it themselves.

5. **Time:** Hope Meadows kids can't be perfect, and they can't get rid of all of their problems and fears overnight. It simply takes time for them to adjust and basically start over.

6. **Security:** Kids here need to feel secure in their home and sur- roundings. They need to know that they are going to always have a home and that their parents will be there for them. Kids need permanency in their lives. That's one of Hope's goals.

7. **Praise:** Some kids have never been told that they've done a good job or that they are worthy of praise. It takes less time to praise than to criticize.

8. **Discipline:** Kids must know what is acceptable and what is not. When you discipline them, you are showing that you love them and they need to understand that, too.

9. **Self-esteem:** Many of the kids who come here have never been taught to feel good about themselves. Some have only been put down and called names or ridiculed. They need to be taught that they are somebody and they can do what they set their minds to do.

10. **Pride:** Hope Meadows kids often have to learn to take pride in their accomplishments and in themselves. Many blame themselves for the things in their lives that brought them here. They need to know that what others have done to them, or not done for them, is not their fault. They should be able to hold their heads up high and be proud of who they are.

It doesn't matter who you talk to. Parents. Foster grandparents. Kids. Staff members. Nearly everyone in the Hope Meadows community has a Debbie Calhoun story. Her name comes up sooner or later in most conversations about the neighborhood. Debbie Calhoun calls once a day just to see if they need anything. She brings groceries. She gives them a ride to the doctor's office. She watches their kids while they take care of an emergency. She sends her kids to help. She brings over doughnuts, a meat loaf, a roast.

It's not like she has nothing else to do. Debbie and Kenny Calhoun have nine children, ages two to twenty-three. They include Mark, Marquis, Kimberly, Jaimie, Marty, Shana, Tina, Darion, and Shaylyn. Seven of them still live at home. Seven are former foster children who they've adopted. Three are teenagers. Five are under the age of ten.

You'd think the woman in charge of such a large household would be unable to see beyond the thicket of Little Tikes toys and heaps of laundry, but Debbie, forty-two, is a one-woman Neighborhood Watch. She is short, with cropped blond hair, keen blue eyes, and maternal urges that register on the Richter Scale. Debbie becomes flabbergasted when asked to estimate how many of her neighbors she checks in on during her typical day: "At least six or seven, on average, I guess. That's either on the phone or in person. I like to check on the seniors who live alone just to make sure they are feeling all right. I don't look on it as a job or anything. I'm just concerned about them because they are my neighbors. It's just the way I was raised."

My mom, who died twelve years ago, was the same type of person. She would do without in order to give to somebody else, and I guess I follow in her footsteps that way. If my brother and sisters had friends who were down and out and needed a place to stay, my mom would put them up and help them out any way she could, even though she didn't have that much herself. She was always taking things to people and doing things for them. It was just part of who she was. Kenny's dad was the same way, and he has followed in his footsteps, too. He and his brothers are known for helping anybody and everybody. They'd give away their last dollar to help another person. So, we have a tradition of helping people in this family, and now I'm seeing our kids following it. It's natural to them. We don't preach that they should go and help, it's just something they do because that is how we live.

The Calhouns' compassion for abused and neglected children, and their instinctive grasp of what they need, is rooted in their own childhood experiences, they said. Debbie's parents divorced when she was three years old. She was ten when her mother remarried and moved from Oklahoma to a mobile home park in Rantoul, where her stepfather worked at Chanute Field as an instructor for the Air Force. By her account, the stepfather was a cruel and abusive man. The marriage ended after just two years. That experience left Debbie with a high level of empathy for children who have suffered at the hands of adults.

Kenny Calhoun's boyhood home is just a few blocks from the former Chanute Field Air Force Base. He has five brothers and two sisters. Their parents split up when he was nine years old and his father got custody of the children. Since his father worked in his dry cleaning stores and his barbecue restaurant until late at night, Kenny and his brothers were left to fend for themselves most of the time. "We washed our own clothes and took care of the house, and the responsibility made me a better person."

Kenny is a plant operator for the city of Rantoul's water department, and has occasionally held down a second job on the night shift at a halfway house for juvenile offenders. Like his wife, Kenny is also an unofficial goodwill ambassador at Hope Meadows. His Friday night barbecues in the summer months are open to all, and a major social event within the community. Tall and burly with a deep, booming voice, Kenny is a strong presence. But his genial nature is not to be mistaken for a lack of convictions. He is a fierce advocate for his young charges, and has a low tolerance for those who don't meet their responsibilities as parents, or members of the community.

My father was very active in the community and I get it from him. His name was William T. Calhoun, but everybody knew him as "Smokey." He was a leader and a great role model. He served as a member of the citizens' advisory board to the city, and he was active in the church. He was known for getting things done. Once they were having problems with people not taking care of their property in our part of town and he put together a huge community cleanup and got everyone to pile all of their junk in their front yards and the city picked it up. He was always a very hard worker, but if I needed him, he was there. He would lecture us for hours and hours, and I took a lot of stuff he told me and remembered it. He'd lecture on everything from sports to girls, the dos and don'ts of life. There was nothing we couldn't talk about even when I became a grown man.

My father was always involved in my life. He taught me the importance of being a role model, particularly as a black man. I don't know what's happened over the last thirty years, but the black community used to be a lot closer. It used to be that if you got out of line when your parents weren't around, there was always somebody willing to step in and set you straight, and then call your parents about it. Now nobody is willing to step in. It used to be if a parent died, or wasn't doing the job, family members would step in. That doesn't happen as much anymore, which is why there are so many kids in foster care. Too many people are just out for themselves now. And that's a sad thing.

A lot of people praise us and tell us that we are doing a good job and that's fine, but basically I'm here for the children and my reward is seeing them growing up to be outstanding citizens, to be the best they can be. I'm not looking for any praise or rewards for taking these kids. God will take care of my reward. The main thing is that I get to see these kids grow up and get out on their own. We have at least one daughter, maybe two, who will be basketball stars, but that's not what I'm talking about. I'm talking about them growing up to be hardworking, good, honest people who don't have a chip on their shoulders. One day I'll be able to look at them and say, "Hey, I had something to do with their success in life." That's my reward. I know my wife and I will be a part of their lives.

It's our calling from God to be here and to take care of children, and I don't see that calling ending. Our plan is to stay here, raise our children until they are old enough to be on their own, and then we'll probably move to an apartment and become foster grandparents here. I don't think this job is ever going to end, and that's fine with us. We have a good life here.

Debbie, who is white, and Kenny, an African-American, have been together sixteen years. They are such kindred spirits that their racial differences hardly register with those who know them. "Our kids never talk about it and neither do our friends," said Debbie. "I guess because we've been in this community so long, and because Hope Meadows is a multiracial neighborhood anyway, it just doesn't matter." What does matter, Debbie said, is their commitment to providing a stable and supportive environment for needy children.

We try to put ourselves in their place. How would you feel if you were moved from one place to the next? I've heard many horror stories about what has happened to these kids in their own homes and in foster care, too. I've seen the bruises and the broken bones. I really don't know how people can hurt an innocent child. When we first got Darion, he went through withdrawals from 10:30 at night until 1 A.M. for five or six months. I could set my clock by it. The doctor said it was likely that his mother shot up at that time of the night while she was pregnant. That's when she got her fix, so that is when his body wanted it, too. He screamed and screamed and screamed. We'd swaddle him in a blanket and hold him tight, but you really can't give them anything to relieve the pain. They have to work their way through it. It lasted about two and a half hours every night. He'd be so exhausted, then he'd sleep most of the day, but he'd get the shakes periodically. He was constantly throwing up and drinking excessive amounts of formula because he didn't get enough nutrients when his drug-addicted mother was carrying him.

I can't imagine what most of these kids have gone through. I don't have much sympathy for their parents when they are taken away. If parents can't get their lives together for the good of their kids, I don't feel sorry for them. That may sound harsh, but the courts usually give them a year or two before they will take the kids away and they have access to all sorts of help. If their priority is still taking drugs or drinking, or whatever, well, I'm sorry, but these kids deserve better.

Kenny and I have been taking in kids for more than ten years and we've never gone away together for a weekend because we feel that it's our responsibility to be here for these kids. We both love kids and we want to provide them with a nurturing home. It's just hard to say no when another child needs a place to go. As a young girl, I never would have dreamed that I'd have a house full of them, but now that's what our life is built around. In the beginning, we were just foster parents and

I had no intention of adopting, but once you have had them in your home and you know their own parents have given up rights to them, you can't just open the door and throw them out. You want to give them permanence.

When we were taking in kids temporarily, I'd try to build up an emotional wall so I wouldn't get too attached to them and feel a loss when they had to leave, but that is not easy for me to do. You can deny that you are feeling that way, but you can't escape it. It is too hard for me to be wondering where they are and if they are doing all right. And, I don't want the other kids in our house to always be wondering when their turn will come, when they'll be walking out the door.

The Calhouns became licensed foster parents in 1989, and moved to Hope Meadows when it opened in 1994. They have served as guardians for nearly thirty children over the years. The couple has faced many challenges in caring for cast-off, abused, and neglected children. Three of their adopted children are siblings who came from a family of thirteen children, all of whom were taken into the foster care system. Before child welfare authorities stepped in, the two oldest in that sibling group were taking turns going to school and watching their younger siblings because their mother was never around. They never got the chance to be kids and they resented that. Two of the Calhouns' youngest adopted children were born with drug addictions, and went through withdrawal while in their care.

In spite of all the cruelty they experienced early in life, the Calhoun children are among the most well-regarded at Hope Meadows, and their gregarious, big-hearted parents are pillars of the community. "Brenda said that she would never allow us to move away," said Debbie. Their dedication to needy children is powerful, but it was put to the test early in their days as foster parents before they came to

Hope Meadows. "With those first two foster kids, I was ready to turn in my license as a foster parent," said Debbie.

The two brothers were eight and nine years old. According to their case files, they had been sexually abused for at least five years. When they were placed with the Calhouns at their home in Rantoul, the boys begged to be returned to their birth mother because they'd come to crave the abuse inflicted by a friend of the family. The children were consumed with sexual thoughts and impulses that therapists, counselors, psychologists, and psychiatrists could not seem to diminish. "We went through counseling, play therapy, role modeling, nothing worked. We had them for a year and a half and we couldn't take in any more kids while we had them. It was like we lost that whole period of time that we could have been helping other kids," said Debbie.

You wouldn't believe the things they did and how they acted out. One morning, we heard noises in the bathroom and we got up to discover that they had cut holes in the heater vents so they could watch me getting undressed and taking baths. It's sad because it is not their fault. They didn't do anything wrong. They'd just been abused so long they didn't know any other way to behave. I don't think we failed with them. They were beyond us. DCFS admitted that they should not have been in foster care. They should have been institutionalized, which is where they ended up. Unfortunately, I see those kids hurting someone someday. I don't think the damage done to them can be undone. I can see them continuing the pattern, the abused become abusers unless somehow the pattern is broken.

Breaking self-destructive and antisocial behavioral patterns in abused and neglected children is one of the two primary challenges of Hope Meadows parents, seniors, and staff. The second challenge is establishing new and more acceptable patterns of behavior in young people who often have had no positive role models in their lives. The Calhouns appear to have had considerable success in meeting both challenges. Their ten-year-old son Marty, for example, came to them as a "temporary" foster placement at the age of thirteen months. His birth mother and father were both in prison on drug convictions. When he was removed from his birth parents' home, a caseworker's assessment of the boy said that he was "failing to thrive." Today, Marty does have some learning disabilities, but his people skills and his concern for others are the stuff of neighborhood legend. The senior residents of Hope Meadows hail Marty Calhoun as "the mayor of Hope Meadows." They say he is the kid to call when you need the trash taken out, your car washed, or just some good company at the dinner table.

"Marty is always there willing to help," said Al Pena. "He rides his bicycle around looking for people moving in or out and he volunteers to help them. He'll work all day if that's what it takes. Even when he was six years old, he'd carry the gas can around for me when I was Weedwacking around the neighborhood. Just yesterday, he was out helping the maintenance man spread mulch. He's the only kid out here who will volunteer to help rake leaves, too."

Another senior, Bill Biederman, noted that the chunky, bespectacled boy keeps a close tab on everyone and everything going on in the community. "He'll help you do anything, or he'll sit and talk to you for thirty or forty minutes. When he was younger he'd talk to you most of the day if you wanted the company, but he's a little busier now."

No activity in the neighborhood goes on without Marty's input,

Biederman said. "A couple years ago, a city crew was looking for a gas leak out here. Marty wanted to watch so I took him over and I explained that they could only dig so far with their heavy machinery and then they'd have to dig by hand to avoid making a spark and possibly triggering an explosion. Well, the workmen went off to lunch and we left, but later in the day I went back over there and one of the workmen said, 'Who was that boy with you?' When I asked why, he said that Marty had come back on his own and told the crew just how they needed to dig for that leaking pipe without causing an explosion. He remembered everything I told him and then repeated it back to them."

The Calhouns' precocious son is not above using his intimate knowledge of the inner workings of Hope Meadows to his advantage. On evenings when his mother's dinner table offerings do not exactly match his tastes, Marty has been known to patrol the neighborhood, stopping to sniff at the exterior vents of the kitchen exhaust fans at each residence. When he finds a scent that whets his appetite, he may just invite himself to dinner.

Not that Mayor Marty ever lacks for invitations. "He's such good company that people are always asking him to go places with them. I just took him to a Fighting Illini basketball game because my daughter and husband couldn't go," said Carolyn Casteel, the office administrator at Hope Meadows. "I know a lot of the seniors ask him out to dinner when they don't feel like eating alone. He's just a very curious, helpful, and caring kid."

Five years after Debbie and Kenny Calhoun began parenting the toddler who had been "failing to thrive," widowed Hope senior Irene Bohn answered the doorbell in her apartment down the street from the Calhouns' home. She found Marty standing on her doorstep.

"Do you live alone, Grandma?" he asked.

"Yes, I do," Bohn replied.

"Your husband's dead?"

"Yes, he is."

"Did you kill him?"

"No."

"Did he get real sick?"

"Yes, he did."

"Do you miss him?"

"Yes."

"Do you cry?"

"Yes."

"Well, I'm going to come and live with you."

"You are?"

"Yes, you need a man in the house."

That night, Debbie Calhoun reports, she found her six-year-old adopted boy intently packing his suitcase, fully intending, it seemed, to carry on the Calhoun family's caring tradition and a new pattern of behavior born of a caring community.

If you wish to join or support the work of Generations of Hope at Hope Meadows, you can contact them at:

Generations of Hope
1530 Fairway Drive
Rantoul, Illinois 61822
Attention: Carolyn Casteel

Their Web site is Generations of Hope.org.

Generations of Hope is a tax-exempt, nonprofit agency, organized under the laws of the state of Illinois and tax-exempt under section 501(c)(3) of the Internal Revenue Code.